FOLLOW
THE
MODEL

FOLLOW THE MODEL

MISS J'S GUIDE TO UNLEASHING
PRESENCE, POISE, AND POWER

J. ALEXANDER

G

GALLERY BOOKS

NEW YORK LONDON TORONTO SYDNEY

G

Gallery Books
A Division of Simon & Schuster, Inc.
1230 Avenue of the Americas
New York, NY 10020

First Gallery Books trade paperback edition July 2010

GALLERY BOOKS and colophon are trademarks of Simon & Schuster, Inc.

For information about special discounts for bulk purchases, please contact Simon & Schuster Special Sales at 1-866-506-1949 or business@simonandschuster.com.

The Simon & Schuster Speakers Bureau can bring authors to your live event. For more information or to book an event contact the Simon & Schuster Speakers Bureau at 1-866-248-3049 or visit our website at www.simonspeakers.com.

Designed by Jaime Putorti

Manufactured in the United States of America

10 9 8 7 6 5 4 3 2 1

Library of Congress Cataloging-in-Publication Data
Alexander, J. (Runway coach)
   Follow the model : Miss J's guide to unleashing presence, poise, and power / J. Alexander.
      p. cm.
   1. Alexander, J. (Runway coach) 2. Models (Persons)—United States—Biography. 3. Fashion—Biography. 4. Success. I. Title.
   HD8039.M772U535 2009

   650.1082—dc22   2009019939

   ISBN 978-1-4391-4990-4
   ISBN 978-1-4391-5051-1 (pbk)
   ISBN 978-1-4391-6517-1 (ebook)

this book is dedicated to:

My late grandmother, Sadie Grant Cohen Carter, who taught me the value of a dollar and allowed me to use her sewing machine pre-drag.

Who gave birth to my late mother, Mary Elizabeth Cohen Jenkins, who gave birth to me and allowed me to be post-drag.

And, finally, to my late father, Julius Montrolius Jenkins, who saw the vision before I did and said, "Boy, you are so damn crazy. If I was rich I would put you on TV."

Well, Pops, I'm on TV. And it cost you nothing, just your support.

> Love,
> Your son and grandson,
> Alexander
> a.k.a. J. Alexander
> a.a.k.a. "Miss J"

CONTENTS

INTRODUCTION

There's no getting around it—the church is the reason I am who I am today. I thank Jesus I ended up a man with a killer stride that has the power to burn footprints into a runway.

I learned the golden rules that every human being needs to know while attending St. Augustine Catholic Church in the Bronx with my mother, but it wasn't the sermons that changed my life.

It was my christening gown.

The dress was a gorgeous, duchesse satin ivory affair, covered in lace and a matching lace bib. The outfit came accessorized with a tiny coordinating hat and slippers, one of which I still have to this day. (The prince still hasn't shown up though.)

Catholics know how to dress for an occasion. Yet,

even as a baby, looking out over that congregation, I sensed I was the classiest-looking person in the room. I hate to brag, but I put every lady in her flowered Sunday hat to shame.

That was my first coming-out party. It would have been perfect but for one little mishap: On my christening certificate, my name appears incorrectly. Instead of Alexander Jenkins, someone had spelled it Alexa*nerd*.

I told you they were jealous.

Looking back at that major moment in my early life, it's no wonder I ended up a six-foot-four black man with a love for the look of fine gowns and an encyclopedic (yes, almost nerdlike) knowledge of the fashion industry. From the second I popped out of my mother's womb I knew I was meant to be someone. And I sensed I was meant to share everything I've learned along the way with the world. So sit back with me, kick up your heels, and let me teach you a thing or two about life, work, love, and of course, fashion.

And just for fun, let's see if I can do it without once mentioning the word *fierce*.

CHAPTER ONE

MOTHER KNOWS BEST

I was born April 12 at 10:10 AM and I moved straight into our family home on Clinton Avenue in the Bronx. I was number seven of ten kids. In birth order there was: Barbara Ann, Ronald, Steven, Stanley, Beverly, Reginald, me, Phillip, Phyllis, and Valerie.

My family is one-eighth Jewish on my grandmother's side, so I won't blame something like Catholicism for my mother's house full of kids. I think it's more that my parents were deeply and madly in love with each other and liked to express that affection in, well, the most *elemental* way.

Sometimes, to my dismay, quite loudly.

Despite the amount of love in that house, from the beginning we were like the Kennedys of the South Bronx. There was always some sort of horrific tragedy besetting us. My mother, Mary Elizabeth Cohen Jenkins, buried six of her children before passing away herself. At age ten, Reginald fell and never recovered from a concussion. Barbara Ann died of breast cancer at age twenty-three. Steven left us at age forty-four from an aneurysm. My baby sister Valerie died of AIDS at age twenty-nine. Stanley died of a heart attack at age forty-eight, and Ronald died too young, at age fifty-four, from throat cancer. Consider this my first bit of advice—*don't smoke.*

My family is like some Greek tragedy come to life, with characters dying off left and right. I don't mean to sound callous or flip about it, but it's a fact of my life that I've experienced a lot of loss. I've had to learn to mourn and move on. I'm a firm believer that you *must* move on. I'll get more into this philosophical stuff later.

Growing up, my mother ruled our house like a five-foot-three-inch dictator. She could be very strict and, let's say, "physically communicative" if she felt she was being disrespected. But I don't mean that in a bad way. It never had to do with her being a mean or evil person. She was simply scared that if one of us kids disrespected *her,* then we would feel it would be okay to go out into the world and disrespect others. If you were breaking rules in the house, she was afraid it meant you would break laws out in the real world and end up in jail. She wanted to raise us better than that. If it took an occasional wallop upside the head to get that lesson through, well, that was just her way. And to be perfectly honest, it worked. Not that I'm advocating anything.

Dinner was at seven o'clock every night, no matter what. There were too many mouths to feed, so there had to be some order to the chaos. She would always set a place for every single child in the house. If you missed the seven o'clock sit-down, you missed dinner completely. The first chance was your only chance. If any of us missed more than one meal, we'd sneak into the kitchen for a bowl of Cap'n Crunch or Froot Loops after everyone had gone to bed.

Raising children can be like raising dogs. You have to lift up your voice to let them know who's in charge. When a dog is fighting in the street, it's fighting for power and control. It's the same thing when a child throws a tantrum. Kids will test the boundaries constantly. And my mother made sure we failed that test every single time, at least until we were old enough to make our own decisions and choices.

My father kept out of all of this though. Julius Montrolius Jenkins was a quiet man and mostly stayed to himself. He worked at the Humboldt Dye Works and would get up every day, Monday through Friday, at four thirty AM to head out of the Bronx and into Brooklyn, in rain, sleet, sunshine, heat wave, or snowstorm. He'd bring his hard-earned paycheck back home to Mother, keeping just a little bit in his own pocket for hanging out with his best friend, Mr. Sol, who owned an auto repair shop in Hunts Point. On weekends, my father would help Mr. Sol fix cars and drink cocktails, and every Sunday, he would sleep in and watch sports all day.

My father was the go-to man in our neighborhood whenever tax time came around. He did everyone's returns for them and got paid either a bottle of scotch, a very small amount of cash, or nothing at all. Despite his selflessness, for some reason he wasn't a physical man that any of us hugged. Yet he was a verbal man, and when he spoke, we listened. But our mother ran our lives. That's not to say that I didn't love him. I did, very much. But for the most part he left the parenting to my mother. He always deferred to her when it came to house rules or handling us when we broke the rules, of which she had many.

A good example is her feelings about house parties. We children were never allowed to go to a house party under any condition. I suppose because inside a house there are closets that you can disappear into for Seven Minutes of Heaven and empty bottles everywhere, just waiting to be spun. One night, when I was in the sixth grade, my parents went out with some friends, and I snuck out of the house. A girl down the street was having what we called a "pay party." In order to get inside, girls had to pay thirty-five cents, boys had to pay fifty cents, and couples had to pay seventy-five cents. I was positive that I would make it back home before my parents.

The party was everything you want a party to be at that age. It was packed with kids from my school, the music was fantastic, and all night long I was lost in the embrace of a slow dance with a beautiful girl. I don't remember her name but I remember the band that was playing was called Black Ivory. When what was about to happen happened, I was, shall we say, aroused. (Yes, I was attracted to a girl. It's actually perfectly normal. Don't judge me.)

I was young, I was happy, and I was in a state of sexual bliss when suddenly the needle on the record screeeetched across its surface and the room fell silent. Like a scene out of a bad teenage comedy, the room suddenly filled with harsh light from above and I froze like a cockroach revealed on a kitchen counter. All I heard was a little girl's frightened, trembling voice whisper, "H-hello, Miss Mary."

My mother stormed into the crowd of kids, grabbed my arm, literally gave me a kick on the butt and a smack on the head, and told me to "bring my black ass" out of there. She dragged me across the room and headed to the door, and as we passed the little girl whose house it was, she looked at her, nodded curtly, and said, "Say hello to your momma for me," and flicked the light switch back off for the rest of the partygoers.

I guess that's why they call it "tough love." She was tougher than the hide of an Hermès Birkin bag. It didn't matter if you were her son or her daughter; she treated all of us the same and didn't play favorites.

Many people I know in the fashion community have strong mothers, too, and in a way, I think many people who dress in drag are trying to emulate or honor that early defining presence they knew. Whether the relationship is good or bad, strong women tend to leave an undeniable impression on their children, one that shapes their attitude or dress. Or in my case, both. My mother was a major fashion inspiration. Though she often wore simple housecoats with penny loafers—and usually had a Pall Mall Gold in one hand and a small glass of scotch in the other, with an empty Hellmann's

Listen To Your Mother!

*Y*ou may think your mother is an overbearing hassle when she calls you five times a day to check up on you, but trust me, her ulterior motive is to help mold you into a better person. What you see as a crazy woman never leaving you alone and wanting to get into every little bit of your business is in reality just a woman who wants the best for you and will do anything in her power to make it happen. (Well, in most cases. I fully admit there are some total crazies out there, too.) Even though I was mortified when my mother burst into my friend's party and dragged me away, looking back I can see she was just trying to keep me in line because I had recklessly broken the rules she set for us children.

my formidable but always fashionable mother.

mayonnaise jar full of ice water nearby to use as a chaser—she could dress up *fabulous* when she wanted to. I remember looking at chic pictures of her from the fifties and sixties. In her wedding photographs she wore a perfectly tailored navy blue coat with an off-white lining that had big hand-painted navy blue flowers. One day I found her wedding dress in her closet, and when I pulled it out I discovered that the print was repeated on the dress itself. She had paired it all with navy pumps and a pillbox hat with an ivory veil. It was a classic look, yet still a bit daring since it wasn't a traditional wedding dress. My mother certainly knew how to make an impression when she wanted to, both in the way she dressed and the way she acted. I definitely inherited those strengths from her.

The first time she discovered me in her closet, rifling through her Sunday best (or as she called them, "my going-out clothes"), she had a fit and started screaming, "Stay out of my goddamn closet! Playing in my good clothes—what, you want to be a girl?" I remember thinking, *Hell no, I just want to wear nice, pretty things.* She was the one who told me that pink was for girls and blue was for boys. I wanted to know which jerk made up that stupid rule. But for years when I was young I separated the two colors in my mind. In fact, when I first started playing dress-up with my sister Barbara's clothes, I was drawn to yellow, because I thought it was a color with no gender. I'd wear one of Barbara's old Easter dresses with a crown made of paper and make-believe that I was a fairy princess. I felt *beautiful* but my brothers would tease me mercilessly. It seemed so unfair. More than anything I wanted to be beautiful. It wasn't about being a woman; I just wanted to live inside the fantasy that women's clothes afforded. I still don't have any desire to be a woman. (But I suppose if I *had* to be one, I'd like to be a woman of the 1950s with a tight waist, large bosom, and a big skirt. Or maybe a 1920s flapper.)

Halloween became an incredibly important holiday for me as a kid, because it was the one time where I could wear a dress and not get teased. The first year I discovered this, I dressed up in Barbara's beautiful graduation dress. It was white lace, with a full skirt below the knee, long sleeves, and a jeweled neckline. I slipped on a pair of white wingtip Mary Janes with two-and-a-half-inch heels, filled up an empty bottle of Johnnie Walker Red with iced tea, and went trick-or-treating as a drunk bride.

I think back on my childhood as a generally happy time except for one thing—we couldn't afford the things I really wanted. At the beginning of each school term my mother would sit back in her armchair, light up a cigarette, and look at the newspaper circulars for sales. When I was eleven years old, right before the beginning of the sixth grade, she picked up the latest newspaper and started flipping through it. By this time she was an expert and quickly found what she was looking for.

"Okay, here are some pants for $7.99, and some shirts for $4.99, and a pair of shoes for $10. Get two pairs of the shirts and pants and one pair of shoes. That should do you." This was the first time I had been allowed to do the shopping on my own, so she opened her purse, got out her wallet, and gave me some cash and the stink eye, telling me to get *exactly* what she told me to and that I'd better bring back the change and the receipt.

Well, I knew how to handle this. I was already extremely tall for my age, so the lie about how none of the pants that I tried on fit me would come easily enough. I figured I could also say something about how the crush of frenzied consumers made it impossible to shop, that the crowds had already picked over everything that was on sale.

I had to lie and scheme, you see, because I had my eye on a pair of $25 shoes. To this day I remember them vividly, every detail. The brand was Thom McAn. They were lace-ups with burgundy leather sides, a black center, and stacked wooden heels.

My plan almost worked. I got one cheap pair of pants and one inexpensive shirt and spent the rest of the money on the shoes. When I got home, my mother nearly believed my story, until she asked for the receipt and change. I had totally forgotten I was supposed to bring proof back with me. I just looked around pretending to be confused and said, "Huh? What receipt? Look, I got shoes."

Well, Mary Elizabeth Cohen Jenkins narrowed her

eyes and got a closer look at my shoes, instantly realizing what I had done. She made me take *everything* back to the store and return her money. Because of my attempted trick, there were *no* new clothes for me at all that semester. It was right then and there that I knew if I wanted things in this world, I was going to have to go out and get them myself. I would do whatever it took to make enough money to get my own clothes.

So I got a job delivering *The New York Times*.

Now, this was no little white-boy job in the suburbs, where I was riding around on a red bicycle with cards in the spokes, streamers on the handlebars, a golden horn, and a basket full of rolled-up papers to toss at someone's perfectly manicured lawn. (That said, at least I delivered the *Times*. I had taste, even then.) This was the hood and I had a shopping cart. I worked my butt off every weekend. And as proud of me as my mother was, she worried about me being out there alone. We lived in a rough neighborhood and newspaper boys have to carry cash on them on collection day. My mother always told me to stand up for myself. If a gang came after me, I was to make sure there was a wall behind me so no one could sneak up. And she told me to *always fight back*. Because once someone realizes they can pick on you, they will continue to do so.

WALK THIS WAY:
Defend Yourself

*A*lways fight back against bullies, whether they're strangers on the street, your roommate, or coworkers, because everything that went down in the South Bronx back then can also easily be applied to everyday situations. The standard suggestion is to ignore a bully and they will go away. I think that idea is for wimps. If you can't stand up for yourself, no on else is going to stand up for you. Whoever is picking on you is going to realize they can continue to do so, and you'll become the whipping post for whatever is going on in their messed-up little mind. No matter how scary it seems, take a stand. Once a person discovers they can attack you without repercussions, they will just keep on doing it. Try to keep your response verbal though; I don't want to be responsible for one of you getting your ass whipped if you can't fight back.

the formidable but always
fashionable me.

I was lucky enough to never get picked on too bad out on the streets. If someone called me a faggot I'd just say, "Yeah, and?" That's about as far as it would go. I think maybe people sensed some sort of toughness in me. Not only was I tall, but I'd already faced down my most formidable opponent on many occasions—my mother. And people could see it in my eyes. But what *did* happen with that first job is that it instilled in me my work ethic. I suddenly had *my own* money to spend on anything I wanted. And the first thing I did was go back to buy that pair of Thom McAns that my mother had made me return.

The day I finally got them, I bought some extra supplies before heading home. I ran straight up to my bedroom and went to work adding taps to the bottoms of the shoes, so they would click everywhere I walked in them. And I walked with a purpose. It wasn't just some *clackity-clack* sound—you could hear me coming from two blocks away on a quiet day, with strong and powerful, even strides. I guess you could say I wanted to be seen *and* heard.

In a way, those shoes were my first pair of high heels.

My older sister Barbara and I were pretty close at this time. She had graduated from high school and was out on her own working at a payroll company. She used to pick me up on the weekends to take me out to restaurants, which was the biggest deal in the world to me. I was so wide-eyed and innocent and it seemed impossibly glamorous to have these people come to your table and ask you what you wanted to eat and wait on you hand and foot. Most of the kids I knew at the time had never even been to a restaurant. It was unheard-of. The idea was, if you can make food at home, why the hell would you go out and pay for it? But Barbara always wanted to treat me. I didn't realize it was because she was dying.

Death Becomes No One

*g*etting over a death is the hardest thing a person will ever have to face. It's important not to bottle up your feelings. You *have* to let yourself go through a mourning period, but you also need to know when it is time to move on. I don't mean to sound callous, but everyone dies, and no one would ever want you to stop living your own life because of that. Everyone deals with the passing of a loved one differently, so do it in the way that works for you, but make sure to try to keep an end in sight. It will never stop hurting completely, but over time it will hurt less. The best way to celebrate another human's life is to live yours to the fullest.

That said, it almost goes without saying that it's so completely normal to feel *absolutely shattered,* not to mention hopeless and withdrawn. But over the years, I have learned that some go through the process, shall we say, more healthily than others. Here are some dos and don'ts for handling overcoming loss:

- Do cry. Don't hold back.
- Do take your time working through complicated emotions. Don't expect that you will be able to function normally again immediately.
- Do notice any change in habits, like excessive eating or loss in appetite.
- Don't ignore the fact that you ate two pints of ice cream in a row or haven't eaten in days.
- Do seek professional guidance. Don't think you need to be "stronger than that."
- Do express your grief verbally. Don't keep everything bottled up inside.
- Do comfort yourself with things that make you feel better.
- Don't turn to drugs and alcohol to cope.
- Do honor a loved one with a beautifully framed photo. Don't hide all of their pictures because you think seeing their image will hurt too much.
- Do lean on others for support. Don't shut yourself away from the world!

No one told me anything. The first time I realized anything was wrong was when one of her breasts disappeared and she began spending a lot of time in the hospital. All I noticed was that her body was changing, but no one would tell me much except that she was sick. I was confused and scared but not exactly worried. I was still a kid and I just didn't realize it was a sign of something much worse.

One day I was sent with my sister Beverly to shop for the week's groceries, and when we returned home one of my neighbors was sitting on the front steps, sobbing. She looked up and noticed me, and said, "I'm so sorry to hear about your sister."

"What?" I asked, totally confused.

"Your sister just died."

All I remember next is screaming, dropping the grocery bags, and running up the stairs to the fifth floor and finding my mother, sitting there, totally numb and in shock. I just held on to her and cried. She remained so stoic and still, but the tears streamed silently down her cheeks.

It was my first experience with death. The funeral was awful. Everyone was crying and I remember thinking I just wanted everything to stop. I went and saw the body. My sister was laid out in her white lace graduation dress in a pearly gray coffin. Her hair was done just like it had been in her high school graduation photo five years before—Shirley Temple curls and a side ponytail. She was wearing peach lipstick. For some reason, that detail is burned into my memory.

I couldn't make it inside the church for the memorial service. I stayed in the car and cried. Grief paralyzed me. I watched them carry the coffin up the steps. But once the terrible day was over, the experience was done for me as well. Over the next few years and then on through the beginning of the AIDS epidemic people began dying all around me. I learned early that you must grieve when someone you know passes away, but once it's done, it's done. There is nothing you can do, so it is best to just move on as well as you can. I don't mean you should forget about them, but there are healthier ways of mourning the loss of a person, like getting involved with a charity if they died of a particular disease. I've walked for breast cancer to raise money in tribute to Barbara. And I've gotten involved in speaking up about AIDS. I've had a huge number of friends, loved ones, and room-mates die from the disease. Recently, Malcolm Harris, a friend who is the founder of the Designers for Darfur campaign, asked if I would come and give a speech at a party called the Latex Ball, which is basically a big annual

How You Too Can Get Involved In Aids And Breast Cancer Awareness

*i*t's no secret that AIDS and breast cancer are two of the biggest killers of men and women on the planet. And like me, chances are your own life has probably been touched by one or both of these devastating diseases. I truly believe that it's very important to take action. Obviously, if you have the money to donate, then good for you. You should, and please do. But since not all of us are flush with cash (trust me, I've been there), you can go online to find out about how you can get involved with spreading the word and fund-raising. Start with Susan G. Komen for the Cure (ww5.komen .org) and/or the United Nations' HIV/AIDS program UNAIDS (www.unaids.org). Additionally, many companies sell fashion and beauty products whose proceeds benefit research funds. (H&M, MAC, Estée Lauder, and Gap immediately come to mind.)

And please, get yourself screened and tested on a regular basis, and always use protection.

voguing competition. I didn't really prepare anything, thinking it would just be a fun lark. When I arrived, I walked out onto the runway and was suddenly confronted with thousands of young gay, lesbian, and transgender kids. I was overcome with emotion, and all of these words came tumbling out of my mouth about how we all have to unite in order to stop the spread of HIV and AIDS. It was all I could do to keep myself from crying, because I didn't want any of these kids to have to face what I did when I was younger and the epidemic first started spreading.

6

CHAPTER TWO

WHITE WOMEN

Right around the same time that my sister Barbara died in 1969, I developed a fascination with white people. I *desperately* wanted to be white. Maybe it had to do with wanting to escape my reality. I saw what white people could afford, how they were treated, and all the opportunities that arose for them just because of their skin color. Sometimes I'd cut school and go up to predominantly white neighborhoods like Riverdale or take the ferry to Staten Island and just walk around, envying the huge houses and beautiful cars. I figured that the white kids who lived in these houses were just like all the white kids I saw on television and were allowed

Vintage clothes are great, but always make sure to wash before wearing. Besides the fact that it's just generally gross not to, in some cases you can even catch crabs!

to do things I would never have been able to get away with.

There was almost always some messed-up white kid on those blocks yelling at their parents out in their driveway. I wanted my parents to get a divorce, just because all the white kids on television had parents who were divorced. Every now and then while I was watching TV I'd see some variation on the exact same scene—a white kid would run up the stairs and slam his or her bedroom door (they rarely shared a room) while screaming, *"I hate you! I hate you! I hate you!"* There were so many times in my life as a kid when I wanted to do that exact same thing to my mother. Rebellion is a perfectly normal part of being a kid. But there was no way I could have ever gotten away with something like that in my house. If I ever even dared to raise my voice at my mother, I'd get a knock on the head with whatever happened to be in her hand—be it a rolled-up newspaper, a fan, or a golf club. (Yes, black people did play golf before Tiger Woods. Maybe not at that level, but an attempt was made.)

Once, after a particularly hard bop on the head after I talked back to her, I tried to tell her I was going to call the police and turn her in for child abuse. She just laughed with that evil tone in her voice, picked up the phone, dialed a nine and then a one, and handed the phone to me. I slunk down the hall to my room and did *not* slam the door or scream *"I hate you,"* because I lived in an apartment and there were no stairs to run up like on TV. I was a rebellious teenager, but one who wasn't about to stand up to Mary Elizabeth Cohen Jenkins.

Case in point—I hated to get my afro combed. I wanted to have straight hair so that it wouldn't hurt when I tried to untangle it. My mother would always hit me on the head with a comb whenever she wanted me to get it done. I remember when she told me, "You're not doing it the right way," and then she'd just comb it out so hard I'd be screaming. If I put my hand up to try to get her to stop, she'd knock it away. "Let me comb this hair!" she'd yell. "If you don't, I'll have it all shaved off. We'll take you to Mr. Kirby and have him cut it all off." (Mr. Kirby was our neighborhood barber.) So I'd let her continue and my scalp felt like it was on fire. Normally I would pick out the top only and never comb the roots. "If you want to have long hair, this big old afro, you take care of it!" she yelled. Not too long after that incident, she told me to go get my hair shaped up. So I went to Mr. Kirby, but I only had him trim it. I wanted to keep my big afro. When I came home my mother stared at me and said, "You went to the barbershop?"

"Yeah," I answered.

"I thought you were going to cut it."

"I did."

"Oh, okay." She didn't say another word. A little while later, she said, "I need to run around the corner to the store, come with me." On the way she suddenly stopped in front of the barbershop.

I thought, *Why's she going in here?*

We walked in the door and she said, "Hey, how are you doing, Kirby? Can you do me a favor?" She pointed at me. "Shave it all off. I want it bald as a baby's ass."

I thought I would die. I almost went into cardiac arrest. I started crying, and she said, "Next time, do as I tell you to do." And then Mr. Kirby shaved my head. "If you want that kind of hair, you're going to cut it regularly and keep it properly."

The next day at school I endured taunts like "eight ball" and "Baldylocks."

As tough as the woman was, I knew she wanted the best for us. She told all of us kids repeatedly, "Just finish school. If you don't want to go to college, that's okay. Get your high school diploma, and I'm good. And if you decide to go to college, then even better. Remember, you're doing this for yourself, not for me."

She was right.

Even though it may not sound like it, my mother was

Stay In School

*P*eople will always try to tell you that the things you learn in school are useless for real life. It simply isn't true. I remember being so annoyed that I had to learn the metric system and military time, and I thought I'd never have to use either of them. But lo and behold, years later I ended up living in Paris, where I needed to know both just to live my daily life. You never know when the random things you get taught are going to apply to your own situation. ◢

---

a very loving and nurturing woman who just had another side to her, a tough side that helped keep all of us kids in order. She would tell us that if we were ever going to rob a bank, rob it for a million dollars, not ten, because you're going to go to jail whatever amount of money. "And if you do get caught," she said, "you don't live here." I always loved that advice, but the thing was that I *did* rob a bank, many times, and I did still live there. It was my sister Beverly's piggy bank. I was always shaking it as hard as I could until a bunch of coins slid out of the tiny slot. I never got caught, and that's probably the reason why I loaned Beverly $1,000 when we were older and then never asked for it back.

When I turned twelve years old, my grandfather on my mother's side passed away, and I went to live with my grandmother to help her around the house. When my grandfather first got sick, my grandmother, Sadie Elizabeth Grant Cohen Carter, would always say, "Will you come and live with me if he dies?" I promised I would, and when that day finally came, as devastated as I was, I must admit there was a tiny part of me that thought, *Thank Jesus, I can have my own bedroom now!*

I moved in with her at the Castle Hill projects in the Bronx. This was the beginning of the period of my life when I really began to blossom. Moving out of your home when you're only twelve years old creates a defined sense of independence, even if you're still living with a relative. There was something about breaking that parental control at such an early age that, for me, fostered a sense of independence that has stayed with me this far.

One of the first lessons my grandmother taught me

Frugality Rules

*A*lmost everyone in the fashion business works on a freelance basis, which means that almost half of any paycheck needs to be put away for taxes. Once you take that out, along with agency fees, many hard workers aren't left with much. It's good to learn how to be frugal without being cheap. For example, I love clothes, but being as tall as I am, it's going to cost me extra to get things that come in my size. Since I came from a place of always having to work for what I wanted because I had nothing, it was easy for me to get creative. Since I already know how to sew, I'll pay close attention to the details on luxury labels that I love. A lot of the time I'll see that it's just adding a bit of extra cloth here or shredded something there. So I'll go home and re-create the look myself. Get creative and remember my grandmother's rule about money.

was the value of a dollar. Sure, my mother had tried to drum it into my brain in her own way, but up until that point I had been spending what little money I had on whatever I wanted. But what my wise grandmother advised, and it's a rule I live by to this day, is that for every one hundred dollars you make, you should save $50, spend $25 wisely, and spend the other $25 foolishly. This way you are saving for your future, taking care of your needs, and still letting yourself indulge a bit, which everyone needs to do in order to stay happy and sane.

It's not like my paper route was paying that much anyway, certainly not enough to buy the kinds of clothes that I really wanted. But my grandmother had an old sewing machine, so I moved it into my room, and over time and through a lot of trial and error, I taught myself how to sew. It was tough at first but I eventually got the hang of it.

The styles of clothes I wanted to wear weren't available in the stores that I could afford. But what I *could* afford was fabric and fashion magazines for inspiration. My room at my grandmother's house was soon covered with images ripped from the glossy pages of publications like French and Italian *Vogue*. (Trend-wise, the European magazines always seemed to be light years ahead of

WALK THIS WAY:

Laziness Is A Sin

*i*f you want to learn how to do something, don't sit around and whine and moan, "Oh, I wish I knew how to fly a plane, or cook, or kickbox." These skills are never going to come to you unless you get off your butt and make them happen yourself. Here's a little secret that's even better than that book *The Secret*—living a happy and fulfilling life by making a living out of something you enjoy doing can be boiled down to the same three words that are in every single Nike ad. *Just do it!*

the American ones—I could see that even at a young age.) I was very resourceful; I'd even discreetly rip out photographs of dresses I loved from magazines I found at someone else's house or in the waiting room of a doctor's office.

The first item that I made on my own was a strapless ball gown. It had elastic at the top and a seam down the back, and the waist was encircled with a bow tied in the

these bridesmaid dresses were some of my very first designs.

front. Forgive me, *Project Runway*, but I added a train to the back. With that first dress I didn't even use a pattern, I was just intuitively cutting cloth by feel. I'm a very visual person in that way. You can describe something to me all you want, but until I actually see it, I probably won't get it.

After a few more experiments I felt comfortable enough to make bridesmaid dresses for my cousin Sandra's first wedding. They were mauve satin and had square, straight-cut skirts with slits on the side, chiffon shawls, and flowers on the straps. The maid of honor's dress was a dusty pink color. It was the first time I'd seen any of my creations on anyone besides myself, and it fueled my ambitions. My big inspirations at the time were Valentino, Yves Saint Laurent, and Oscar de la Renta's ball gowns. I was still in my "I want to be white" phase (that's all I could see in American magazines, and despite my love for the European titles, it was hard to escape the influence of what was considered a "classic" American woman). I desperately wanted to be one of those women (like then socialite Pat Buckley) with big hair and glittering jewelry who were going to the Met ball and other glamorous events that seemed to take place in another world.

My family never really paid attention to my budding interest in women's clothing. The only time I ever remember it being brought up openly was when I was hanging out back over at my parents' apartment in the South Bronx one afternoon when I was fourteen. My mother and I were watching the news together when a report came on about protesters from the gay pride parade standing in front of St. Patrick's Cathedral, screaming about intolerance in the church. My mother

Don't Throw It Away, Re-Create It

*S*chools can be very, very cruel for kids who don't have the money for designer or expensive clothes. What you need to remember is that it isn't a label that makes you stand out, it's your individuality. (I was never considered cool because I didn't have designer clothes, plus I looked like a freak in half the stuff I was creating on my own.) Whenever I meet kids who are upset about having to wear hand-me-downs from their older brother or sister, I tell them to make the clothes their own. Belt it, shred it, dye it—do *something* so it looks unrecognizable compared to the original piece. Be creative with what you have. If it's some horrible shirt from the eighties with shoulder pads, take them out and reshape the fabric. You'll have enough fabric to make it look like a slim Dior piece. If you can't sew and don't want to learn how, go to a tailor and tell him exactly what you want. (The best way to choose a good tailor is to just ask to see some examples of their work.) It will still be way less expensive than buying something new. A perfect example is when Elton John had a sale in London of all this stuff he was getting rid of. I went and it was a huge paparazzi fest. I showed up thinking, *He's not as tall as I am.* I saw so many beautiful Versace chesterfield coats in colors like soft smoky blue, wine, navy, mustard, and olive green—all in mint condition. But the sleeves were three and a half inches too short. I'd put one on and think, *I love this coat, it's really great.* Even though it came right above my knees, the body was fine. But I didn't buy it. Despite an incredible bargain price, I thought, *Why buy it? I can't use it, it's too short.* But after I got back home I was mad at myself, because as creative as I am, I should have bought the damn thing. I realized I could have gone to a fabric store and bought solid colors, matched closely to one of those five colors of the jackets, and just added on the additional material in circular stripes to create longer cuffs. Or if I added a few inches of one color to one side and its opposite on the other, it would have made a really great, creative coat. I regret not buying any of those coats to this day. I ignored my own advice. You have to have an artist's eye, be creative, and take risks.

was sitting in her favorite armchair, puffing on a cigarette, when out of nowhere she said, "Lord have mercy, I don't know why the hell they don't leave you boys alone."

Well, I just looked at her like only a young, gay black homosexual can, with a face that had *EXCUUUUUSE ME?* written all over it.

She looked back at me evenly and said, "Well, you are, aren't you? It doesn't change a thing. You're still my child. You just remember that whatever you end up doing in bed, you take it like a man."

Of course it was mortifying at the time, and not just because of the sex reference. I knew who I was, I just didn't think it was something that ever had to be discussed or made a big deal out of. I just thought it was obvious I was gay, to me and everyone else, so why bother discussing it? It certainly wasn't something I felt like I had to go and wear on my sleeve or make a big fuss about.

Around this time I was still delivering the *Times* on Sundays, helping my brother Stanley deliver sodas on Saturdays, and delivering and moving furniture on White Plains Road under the L train after school. (The owner was a Jewish man who always had a big box of black and white cookies inside the store. I'd eat two or

How To Come Out To Your Family

*N*ow, this is a big decision, and no matter how open and accepting your parents are (and let's hope they are), it's never easy. You need to carefully consider the repercussions, especially if you're young and live under your parents' rule: How will this news affect your home life? Are you in a dangerous situation (e.g., physical/emotional abuse)? Do you have resources and external support readily available? If the positives (best: confidence in your identity) outweigh the negatives (worst: majorly unlivable situation), you should make a time and schedule a family meeting and calmly inform your loved ones that you feel they should know where you stand. However, if you realistically assess the situation and ultimately decide that either you or your parents are not ready, then that's totally okay, too. Ideally, you have a close friend and confidant who knows what's up. The most important thing is to feel good about yourself and confident about your sexual identity, no matter what. ⨳

three of them at a time and I'm still hooked on them to this day.) I was already tall for my age, and even though I was skinny, I was starting to develop some pretty nice lean, mean muscles from all the hard labor I was doing. So for the most part people wouldn't mess with me on the street. (Unless I wanted them to!)

standing behind grandma (with corsage) at my cousin's wedding.

Meanwhile, my collection of clothing creations, based on my magazine inspirations, was growing. I was fascinated with one Givenchy ad campaign that used all these black girls on the streets of Paris posing under a lamppost while wearing ball gowns. When I first saw their black, smoky eyes with fuchsia lips and cheeks in French *Vogue*, I remember thinking, *This is major.* I still remember all the models they used—Lynne Watts, Dianne Washington, Sandi Bass, and Carol Miles. There was one black and gold velvet dress in particular that had a white ruffle collar that I was able to re-create. I was a size zero at the time and dresses fit perfectly on me. (Incidentally, Sandi Bass is now a good friend of mine and appeared as a guest judge on the infamous episode of *America's Next Top Model* where contestant Rebecca Epley fainted in front of the panel.)

The more black women I saw in magazines, the happier I became. My productivity level got higher and higher, and it seemed like I was constantly glued to the sewing machine. I loved winters the most, because I could create my craziest concoctions during the colder seasons. All those extra layers one needed to keep warm just meant more opportunities for creating fashion. The clothes I made weren't like actual drag outfits, just more of an outrageous way of dressing. For example, I'd make

Breathtaking Black Models And Their Signature Walks

*L*ong before Naomi Campbell and Tyra Banks, there were Lynne Watts, Dianne Washington, Sandi Bass, and Carol Miles—four women of color who literally took my breath away when they appeared in French *Vogue* during my youthful "fashion awakening." The reason I remember the moment so vividly is because until then, the biggest fashion icons I was exposed to were invariably white. Things have certainly changed over the years, and successful ladies like the aforementioned black supermodels have opened the door for more African-American runway stars to reach the same kind of exposure that white girls usually get.

Still, black models are extremely underrepresented in the fashion world, and while everyone knows who Carol Alt is, Carol Miles is still woefully unknown. People have plenty of theories as to why the industry continues to insist upon predominantly casting white models, ranging from an outdated argument that so-called "ethnic" girls don't sell magazine covers and products to that other nasty, old-fashioned idea: racism, plain and simple. Whatever the case may be, although it can't happen fast enough, the industry *is* changing rapidly. (Witness the storm over size zero being unhealthy and the subsequent emphasis on booking more "plus-sized" girls.) Here's an abbreviated guide to some of the major players whose impact paved the way for more black models to come. Get to know them:

DOROTHEA CHURCH—Total pioneer. After being discovered by Christian Dior, she was the first African-American to infiltrate the Paris fashion scene. She famously said, "If you're beautiful, [the French] don't care what color you are." The Walk: understated and queenlike.

PAT CLEVELAND—Outrageous seventies fashion icon and muse to Yves Saint Laurent and Halston, best known for her charisma and over-the-top poses. The Walk: sexy, slinky, and dancelike.

BEVERLY JOHNSON—Super! Model! The first black woman to be featured on the covers of both American *Vogue* and French *Elle*. The Walk: more editorial than runway, but stunning nonetheless.

SANDI BASS—Model, singer, and television personality, who joined Dianne Washington in the legendary disco troupe Peter Jacques Band (PJB). The Walk: the classic eighties stride, with one hand on the hip, the other arm swinging from below the elbow only.

BILLIE BLAIR—A reed-thin legendary beauty with Modigliani features who took the Halston, Bob Mackie, and Oscar de la Renta runways by storm. The Walk: a dramatic, wiggling sashay.

IMAN—Captured David Bowie's heart. The Walk: the woman literally seems to growl as she prowls. Iman once said, "It's not about the walk, it's about *presence.*"

ARIA—First black girl to do a Ralph Lauren campaign. The Walk: simple and no fuss.

DALMA CALLADO—The Brazilian bombshell enjoyed an infamous rivalry with Iman and competed with her for coveted ranking at Valentino, Bill Blass, and Yves Saint Laurent. The Walk: pure, restrained elegance in heels.

KIMORA LEE—This African-American/Japanese woman and Baby Phat empress was handpicked by Karl Lagerfeld to strut her stuff for Chanel at age fourteen. The Walk: sassy and bold.

TYRA BANKS—First black supermodel to appear solo on the cover of *Sports Illustrated*'s annual swimsuit issue. The Walk: so good that she walked her way into a successful reality show, an Emmy

Award–winning talk show, and a GLAAD award. Need I say more?

ALEK WEK—Perhaps best known for her strikingly dark skin and signature bald head, this Sudanese woman has graced major runways and print editorials. *Major.* The Walk: calm, cool, and collected.

TYSON BECKFORD—One of *People*'s "50 Most Beautiful People in the World" and a VH1 man of the year, he now has his own model-based reality show. The Walk: macho-man strides.

LIYA KEBEDE—She's not only appeared in numerous ad campaigns and on no less than five *Vogue* covers, this Ethiopian goddess is also the first black woman to land a coveted Estée Lauder contract, rumored to be worth an estimated three million. The Walk: languid and catlike.

SELITA EBANKS—This Victoria's Secret supermodel from the Cayman Islands has found mainstream commercial success via *Sports Illustrated* and Ralph Lauren, Tommy Hilfiger, and Abercrombie and Fitch campaigns. The Walk: majorly sexy hip swinging with signature wink at the end.

CHANEL IMAN—She may still be a teenager, but Chanel Iman is no doubt the high-fashion model of the moment and has a long career ahead of her. The Walk: demure but deliberate.

huge bubble tops, where I'd fold fabric up into two large squares, sew up the sides and cut a V in the front, and add a drawstring at the bottom so it had this huge balloon effect. My grandmother was so supportive of me during this time. She'd peek her head inside my bedroom and laugh and say, "I can't wait to see you get rich off of my old sewing machine." That ancient machine never did make me rich, but it definitely helped make me famous.

HOT CHILD IN THE CITY

After I graduated from high school, I spent some time working at my sister Barbara's old place of employment, Payroll Procedures, in midtown Manhattan. The owners of the company remembered me as Barbara's little brother, and I think they felt sorry for me. I was good with numbers, so for a time I even believed I was going to end up an accountant. I shudder to think where I'd be today if that had happened. Imagine hiring *me* to do your taxes.

As fate would have it, I jumped at the chance to make a little extra money working in the stockroom at the Bergdorf Goodman department store, and that's where I

If you're only doing half the eye with your eyeliner, make sure you do the top half, *not* the bottom. A bottom-only line will make your eyes appear droopy.

started hearing about the crazy anything-goes club scene that was taking over the city. The wild stories and pictures I'd see in the newspapers and magazines were like a siren song calling out to me. I knew I had to check it out for myself or I would go out of my mind. I made my first solo journey down to the city's nightlife in the winter, which was convenient for helping me get out of the house in my getup unnoticed.

That first night's escape from the Bronx quickly became a regular routine. I would put the top half of my gown or dress on and hide it under my winter coat. With the rest of my clubbing outfit safely in a garment bag, I'd finish getting dressed in my regular men's pants and winter boots, and then watch for the number 13 bus from my window so I wouldn't have to wait outside in the cold. When I could see it coming I'd jump up and run down twelve flights of stairs to catch it just in time. The bus would take me to the number 6 train at Castle Hill Avenue, which I would take down to 125th Street. I used to see Ms. "Jenny from the Block" Lopez on that same train ride from time to time, heading out to the clubs, too, since we lived in the same neighborhood ("On the 6" indeed). At 125th I'd transfer to the express train and take it down to Fifty-ninth Street, where I'd hop in a cab and start putting the rest of my outfit together during the trip downtown. I'd slip out of my pants and into the bottom half of my outfit, use navy blue or black chalk to do up my eyes, and then cover them with sunglasses. Sometimes I'd use a little bit of white-girl apricot-colored blush and dust my face. I was still teaching myself how to apply the right amount of makeup. It was never a full-on "drag face." Instead, I was going for looks that I saw in my magazines, and I confess my

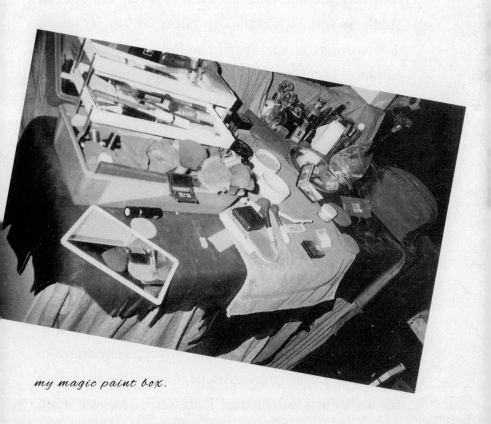

my magic paint box.

experiments often went drastically wrong. (Once, while visiting my mother the day after a night out, she asked, "What's that all over your face?" I hadn't wiped all the chalk off properly, so I just played dumb.)

Transformed, I'd slip the rest of my male clothes into the garment bag just as the cab would pull up to Studio 54 and step out of that taxi like Grace Kelly. The crowds would part and I was always, *always* immediately ushered in. Everyone talks about how tough the door at Studio 54 was back in the day, but really, all you had to do was dress the fabulous part and you'd gain immediate entrance. I suppose it helped to be tall, black, male, and wearing a gown. Inside, I'd check my garment bag and survey the scene. There would be Bianca Jagger, Halston, Liza Minnelli, Jerry Hall, and all the famous names of the time. The busboys wore tight shorts and sneakers and nothing else. The coat-check girls had big teased hair and everyone had big perms with lots of eye shadow, black smoky lids, and red lips. I was in homo heaven.

That first night I showed up alone at Studio 54, but it didn't take very long to make friends. When you look like I do, there are types of people, especially people with a love for the club scene, who are just naturally drawn to you and want to be your friend. One of the first close friends I made was named John Kerins. He was from

Studio 54 For Dummies

*E*ven if the legendary club was *waaaay* before your time, or if, say, you've been living under a rock, here's a quick history lesson and a guide to the out-of-control, outrageous cast of characters that made Studio 54 special. Located at 254 West Fifty-fourth Street in Manhattan, "the Studio," as it was called, was originally an opera house and eventually became a CBS studio. But none of its incarnations were ever as grand as the one that a group of entrepreneurs (including a young Ian Schrager) opened on April 26, 1977; it would become the most memorable, fabulous, chic club in the history of New York nightlife, period. In fact, the first night's list of attendees reads like a Who's Who of the most rich, famous, and powerful people of the twentieth century: Mick and Bianca Jagger, Salvador Dalí, Liza Minnelli, Jerry Hall, Diana Vreeland, Margaux Hemingway, Janice Dickinson, Mikhail Baryshnikov, Brooke Shields, Francesco Scavullo, Martha Graham, Debbie Harry, Robin Leach, Donald and Ivana

Trump, Rick Hilton, and Kathy Richards—and that's just a few of the boldface names. If that doesn't sound extreme enough, Cher, Warren Beatty, Woody Allen, Diane Keaton, and Frank Sinatra (!) were left out with the other hordes of people unlucky enough not to make the cut and get inside. (Now maybe you can see why I was so blown away the first time I sauntered in!) Then again, one of the main draws of the club was that one of the owners, Steve "Lord of the Disco" Rubell, seemed to relish hand-selecting us glam but not-yet-even-almost-famous "nobodies" and adding us to the mix of well-established, red-hot celebrities, artists, and models. I think that's part of why the Studio and its environment were all so amazing.

Inside the studio was a swirl of fabulous frocks, luscious furs, painted ladies (and boys!), glittering jewels, delicious cocktails, and dancing on dangerously high platform heels, not to mention the de rigueur sex, drugs, and rock 'n' roll. I mean, obviously. My nights spent there were magic, and I could be *anybody*. (Well, anybody but a poor black kid from the Bronx who'd snuck out of his grandma's apartment.)

Of course, all good things must come to an end, and wouldn't you know it, only a scandal of epic proportions—involving money, tax evasion, and drugs—would befit Studio 54. It closed on February 4, 1980, with a party called "The End of Modern-Day Gomorrah." Fun fact: Sylvester Stallone is rumored to have been the last person to buy a drink there. While it did reopen with yet another serious star-studded bash in 1981, it never quite hit such epic proportions (although fledgling performers like Madonna and Run-DMC got their starts there) and closed for good in 1986. It's now home to New York's Roundabout Theatre Company. (Incidentally, former Studio 54 regular Brooke Shields went on to perform the role of Sally Bowles in Roundabout's production of *Cabaret* in 2001.) ◢

Massachusetts and had a place in the city on 107th Street and Broadway, where he used to let drag queens come and live with him when they needed a temporary place to stay. Another friend I made was a guy named Luna, who kept a large cutting board behind his bed's headboard on which he would make dresses for his drag queen friends. I later met Michael Stein at Xenon, a designer friend who I'm still friends with today. He lived

me on the westside highway, modeling not sreetwalking.

in the dorms at Parsons on Union Square, so sometimes I'd stay there with him and we'd get all dressed up and go out together.

If I wasn't staying in the city, then the trip back home to the Bronx was always timed as impeccably as the trip into the city because of the way the transit system ran. I'd usually get home between five and six AM, and I'd always tell my grandmother to make sure to leave the chain off the door so I could get back inside without waking her. But sometimes it would be six AM and I'd be home safe in bed and I'd hear her open the bedroom door and peek in on me to make sure I was okay. I always hated that because I felt like I was disturbing her, even though I knew she was doing it out of love. I'd feel so terrible on the nights I forgot to call her and tell her I was coming home and she'd leave the door locked with the chain. I'd have to knock, and from out in the hallway I could hear her hands shuffling across the wall, holding her up as she felt her way in the dark toward the door. She'd ask if it was me, and I'd say yes, but she'd still always open the door a crack and peek out first before unlocking it.

The best night I ever had out at Studio 54 was the infamous New Year's Eve that Grace Jones performed. It cost

WALK THIS WAY:

Entering A Club

*t*he most important rule is to never show up with a giant mob of people. If you're having a night out with a ton of friends, try to stagger your approach, because there is nothing more annoying to a door person than a swarm of giggling girlfriends, *especially* if they are all dressed the same. (You know who you are.) It's hard for a door person to spot welcome individuality when you're already part of a mob. Always try to wear something to make yourself stand out from your friends. If you're a straight man, you flat-out aren't getting in unless you have at least two or three women for every guy in the entourage. But the same general rule applies, so try to stagger your entrance so you aren't just part of a giant swarm.

$50 to get in and I didn't have that kind of extra cash lying around, so a friend lent me the money. The door cover got you hors d'oeuvres and free drinks. That night Grace wore a gold bikini bottom, gold armbands, and a

Never be rude or obnoxious or try to cut the line, unless someone at the door pulls you out of it. Sometimes there's a legitimate reason for there to be a line at the door, sometimes not, but being polite and looking stand-out fabulous will work every time to help you get in. And remember— *don't humiliate yourself.* If the door person doesn't let you in, don't make a scene or throw a fit. Calmly walk away and find somewhere else to hang out. If you don't, you just end up wasting an hour of your life and letting anger build up. There is nothing worse than a group of people begging a bouncer to let them into a club, or even worse, yelling the dreaded phrase *Don't you know who I am?!* If you're the type of person who would say something like that, then put this book down right now, because I don't even want to talk to you. ◢

zigzag part in her hair. It was pure theater and it nearly blew my mind. Here's a fun fact about that night: Grace had forgotten to add the names of the guys from the band Chic to the door list, and they weren't allowed in.

They were so angry that they drove home and wrote a song called "Fuck Off." The chorus went "Aaaah fuck off!" but was soon changed to "Aaaah freak out!" And just like that, a disco classic called "Le Freak" was born and went on to sell six million copies.

The clubs were my runway training ground. I'd walk straight in, position myself under a spotlight, and dance in that same spot for the rest of the night so I was always illuminated for everyone to see. Or I'd have spontaneous walk-offs with other girls, trannies, drag queens, and fag hags. As I kept getting put on the guest list and invited to more and more parties and events, I soon realized the amount of invites directly correlated to how outrageous I looked. The more effort I put into it, the better the party I'd end up being invited to. So I started amping up my looks, with fake eyelashes, eye shadow, lipstick, heels, the whole bit. But I wasn't just doing it for the party invitations; I honestly just wanted to look like the women I saw in French *Vogue* and *Women's Wear Daily.* In high-fashion magazines you're usually looking at exaggerated images, nothing you'd wear in real life. They are meant as art and inspiration, or so it's said. But I actually wanted to look *exactly* like those models.

For example, the first time I went out in semi-full drag, I took two long strips of green plaid fabric, stitched

Don't Put Off Living Your Life

*W*hen I was sixteen years old, I felt like I should hang around the house a lot in case my grandmother ever needed something. When she realized this was one of the reasons why I stayed in so much, she said to me, "Go out with your friends. You could be in the same room or the same apartment as me, and if a glass of water was needed to save my life, you couldn't get a glass of water in time and come back to me; there's nothing you can do. Go out, have fun. Once I'm gone, I'm gone, and just do what you need to do and what you want to do." What she meant was that when your time is up, your time is up. There is no cheating death. She was obviously being extreme with her glass-of-water analogy, but she truly felt I should be out living my own life rather than waiting around for something inevitable. Still, I always felt guilty whenever I went out after that.

them together, folded them, and stitched the pocket. The result was a huge Victorian collar with ruffles. I then made a pair of matching bloomers out of the same material and wore them over Capezio tights with cowboy boots and a massive green tulle skirt with ribbons. I wore that outfit a few times, and there's even a documentary about Studio 54 where you can see me in it, twirling with pipe cleaners in my hair that I'd wrapped with different-colored ribbons that fluttered around my kinky little afro.

High heels were essential for many of my outfits but they were a massive pain for me. It was impossible for me to find anything in my size (I'm a twelve or thirteen, but for Louis Vuitton, I'm an eleven), but I'd wear them anyway, with my toes hanging out one end and my heel out the other. My feet looked like a baloney and cheese sandwich that was too big for the bread. So it helped to wear long dresses or skirts that covered them. If I was wearing something shorter that revealed my feet, I would wrap my ankles in ribbons and put flowers in my toes to distract the eye.

I had a friend who was making a living doing the windows at Saks Fifth Avenue, and he bought me the largest pair of heels he could find, but they were still too small. I cut out the backs of them so that my heels could stick

cory and me inside studio 54.

out, and I ended up in such terrible pain. They hung out a full half inch, while my toes clutched at the front of the shoes like claws. The heels of my feet would be so high in the air that by the end of the night my arches just screamed. I'd try to put my foot down completely flat and I could barely do it.

That first pair of adapted heels lasted me forever. If I was wearing a red outfit, I'd spray-paint them red. If my dress was silver, the shoes would become silver. You get the picture. Lucky for me, I later discovered that my friend Nancy Giallomeardo made shoes. She loved to use me as her guinea pig and would make custom creations in my size. I, of course, appreciated that. I kept several pairs that she made me and still wear them everywhere to this very day. You know, when I'm grocery shopping or doing laundry—even when I go to bed. (Oops, just kidding about the shopping and laundry.)

Eventually I made enough Manhattan friends from being out at the clubs all the time and looking incredible that I didn't have to make the long trek down from the Bronx. I could get dressed much more conveniently at friends' houses beforehand. There was one straight guy friend of mine named Nicholas who lived on Central Park West with his girlfriend and would always let me get ready at his place. For some reason he loved nothing more than to watch me get all dolled up and then take me out to dinner in full drag with his girlfriend. The deal was he fed me first, and then we'd hit the clubs, because I was the one who could get them in. I had arrangements like that with several platonic gentlemen friends. They would follow me in past the bouncers and I'd head straight onto the dance floor, twirling, twirling to the disco beat.

I was very into walk-offs at this point, mimicking the sickest runway strides I could muster against my friends

WALK THIS WAY:
Everlasting (Sort Of) Heels

*i*f you don't have a whole lot of money but still want to look fabulous, spray-painting your heels different colors to keep on matching them with different clothing options really does work, especially if your dress or outfit can distract the eye away from the shoe as much as possible. You know, in case some nosy friend wants to examine them up close. You'll save a small fortune, even if it is only a temporary option. Another way to make your heels appear especially high-end is to simply paint the bottoms of them red so they look like Christian Louboutins.

inside the clubs. But I was a bit of a snob about committing fully to the drag lifestyle. I didn't want to be an exaggerated woman. I never wanted to be one of those club kids wearing the five-inch platforms and three-inch fake eyelashes and toting a lunch box. As strange as it may sound I had no interest in lip-synching to Diana Ross or Dionne Warwick in drag shows. It just wasn't for me. I

Why pay $1,200 for a pair of shoes when that's rent and groceries for a month in most towns? You can also use nail polish to decorate an old pair of heels with new patterns or designs. Let yourself go crazy. Chloë Sevigny once wore thick kitchen rubber bands on a pair of simple pumps as a fashion accessory and it got written up in *Vogue* as a trend item, so you never know what's going to be a surprise hit. Just follow your fashion instincts and, most important, have fun. Also, remember that when you first try on a pair of high heels, you're usually walking on a store's carpeted floor. Make sure to practice on hard surfaces inside your own home before you debut them, and baby-proof any sharp corners!

wanted to look beautiful and glamorous like a couture model. A lot of the club kids were too clownish or child-ish for me, as opposed to committed to glamour. Not that being six foot four, plus an additional three inches taller in heels and full-on drag, wasn't clownish enough— I like to take the piss out of myself. I wanted smoky eyes, glittering jewels draped everywhere, and earrings that

i often wore long gowns to hide my huge feet.

looked like they cost more than my entire outfit, or like I stole them from the chandelier of a posh hotel lobby.

My day job at Bergdorf was almost as glamorous as going out to the clubs. Bergdorf Goodman is one of the most exclusive department stores in all of New York. It was always filled with celebrities and a lot of the Park Avenue, old-money, ladies-who-lunch crowd. It attracted everyone from Cher to Patti Smith. I initially started out in the stockroom, and it was my job to replace any bought items. So if someone bought two Anne Klein dresses, I would dig around in the stockroom and go out onto the floor and replace them. When the store was crowded, sometimes customers would look to me for help if I was out on the floor. But because I was a stockroom boy, I couldn't ring up their purchases. So I'd help out a customer and then give the sale to the nicer girls on the floor. I started to get so good at it that my boss finally gave me a sales book and taught me how to write out a sales slip. I learned one of the most important lessons I've ever learned in my entire career when I started that part-time sales job. This was back before everything was computerized, and all the sales forms had to be written out by hand, with carbon copies filed in different locations so we could record the tax and the sale and track the shipping orders, what was selling and what needed to be reordered, and how many sizes we had left, etc. Well, one day, early on, I made a mistake with the tax on one of the forms and didn't realize it until the order had already gone out. I was so freaked out by the error that I tried to hide the evidence by ripping up the rest of the copies into tiny little pieces and throwing them away in the office garbage can. But of course the original order form was still in the sales book, so when my boss went to look for the rest of the forms I had to admit my mistake.

Instead of yelling and screaming at me, or worse, firing me, she sat me down. Her name was Marcia Lewin, and she said, "Why didn't you ask me?" I didn't have an answer, but I knew it was because I was scared that I had messed up. And then she told me something that has stayed with me ever since. "You appear to be smarter by asking questions than not asking them at all." It was like being hit with a ton of taffeta. It was so obvious, but I'd never thought of it like that before and I knew she was right. Because when you mess up, you'll usually get busted in the end anyway, but more important, admitting mistakes is one way to learn things. To this day I still know so many people who just try to fake their way through situations because they are too afraid to admit they don't know an answer. There is no shame in not knowing, only in staying ignorant out of fear. (When we're at panel on the first episode of a cycle of *America's Next Top Model* we like to ask girls who say they love fashion who their favorite designers are. Many of them choke and can't name a single person. We'd have

*at a david leigh
fashion show at the
palladium club.*

71

a lot more respect for a contestant if she admitted that she didn't know the names of many designers but that that was the exact reason why she was trying to get on the show—that she wanted to *learn*.)

After our talk I went straight back down to Bergdorf's basement, dumped out the trash can, and spent the next four and a half hours finding and taping every single ripped-up piece of those receipts back together.

A few years ago I worked on the Savannah College of Art and Design's fashion show. André Leon Talley had gotten me involved in working with the school for their annual André Leon Talley Lifetime Achievement Award event, wherein the school recognizes a huge name designer for his or her life's body of work, then puts on a fashion show of all the students' designs. I go down south now every year to help the students prepare for the show and to teach the student models how to walk. One of my old Bergdorf coworkers there was in touch with Marcia Lewin and helped reunite us. The next time I was in New York City, Marcia and I met up for lunch at Bergdorf. I thanked her profusely for the lesson she had taught me. She just laughed and told me she didn't even remember that day, but that it was a lesson that someone else had passed on to *her* before. She was thrilled that it had stayed with me all these years, and *I'll* be thrilled if you take this bit of advice and apply it to your own life.

Sometimes people will try to make you feel bad about not knowing something. If you're with a group of people and they are talking about a designer or a new singer and you've never heard of this person, don't just nod and pretend to go along with the conversation. Stop them and say, "I've never heard of so-and-so, who are they?" For instance, remember that scene in *Showgirls* when Nomi incorrectly pronounces her dress designer's name

demonstrating at the savannah college of art and design's fashion show with andré leon talley.

as "Versayce?" She meant "Versace" but no one was kind enough to set her straight until later in the movie, after the damage had been done. Unfortunately, there are a lot of people in this world who like to take a situation like that one and use it as an opportunity to make themselves feel superior and say something undermining and bitchy, like "You've *never* heard of so-and-so? I'm shocked!" It's a transparent bid to make themselves look cooler in front of others. The next time someone pulls this subtle bit of nastiness on you, look them right in the eyes and say, "The *correct* response to my question is to simply answer it."

Back when I was working at Bergdorf, I tried to spend as much time as I could out on the floor making sales, because it was obviously more glamorous than being stuck in the stockroom all day. Despite the wisdom that Marcia had taught me, nothing could have prepared me for a run-in with a monstrous old-money Park Avenue woman. I was helping her look at clothes and she was fiddling with the security chain on a linen and suede dress. I asked her to be careful because the dress was very delicate, and the chain was snagging on it. She glared up at me and said, "Excuse me, but I've been shopping in this store since way before they let your kind in, let alone work here."

The Fashionista's Pocket Pronunciation Guide

*t*he Victorians rank a close second to the fashion world when it comes to being harshly judgmental. Upon closer inspection, no one is as effortlessly cool as they so desperately make themselves out to be. But it never hurts to appear worldly, sophisticated, and smart when it comes to throwing foreign names around the table, right? In the interest of saving you some *Showgirls*-level embarrassment, here's your A–Z phonetic cheat sheet:

ALBER ELBAZ FOR LANVIN: al-BEAR el-BAHZ for lon-VAN

ANNA SUI: A-na SWEE

BALENCIAGA: bah-len-see-AH-gah

BULGARI: BOOL-ga-ree

CHANEL: sha-NELL

CHLOË SEVIGNY: KLO-ee sev-en-EE

CHRISTIAN DIOR: KREES-tyan dee-OR

CHRISTIAN LACROIX: KREES-tyan la-KWA

CHRISTIAN LOUBOUTIN: KREES-tyan loo-boo-TAWN

COMME DES GARÇONS: cum de gar-SON

COSTELLO TAGLIAPIETRA: coast-EL-lo tah-lee-ah-pee-AY-trah

DONNA KARAN: DON-a KAR-en

DOLCE & GABBANA: DOLE-chay & gab-AH-nah

DRIES VAN NOTEN: DREES vahn NOTE-en (or just DREES)

FENDI: FEN-dee

GIORGIO ARMANI: JYOR-jee-oh ar-MAHN-ee

GIVENCHY: jee-von-SHE

GUCCI: GOO-chee

HERMÈS: air-MESS

HERVE LEGER: er-VAY le-JAY

ISAAC MIZRAHI: EYE-zac miz-RAH-hee

ISSEY MIYAKE: EE-say mee-YAH-kay

JEAN PAUL GAULTIER: zhan paul GO-tee-AY

LES COPAINS: lay CO-pan

LOEWE: LO-ee-VAY

LOUIS VUITTON: lew-EE vee-TOH

MANOLO BLAHNIK: mah-NO-lo BLAH-nick

MIU MIU: mew-mew

NICOLAS GHESQUIÈRE: NEE-ko-la guess-KYAIR

PETER SOM: pee-ter SAHM

PRADA: PRAH-da

PROENZA SCHOULER: pro-EN-za SKOOL-er

RALPH LAUREN: ralf LOR-en

ROBERTO CAVALLI: roe-BER-toe cah-VAHL-ee

SALVATORE FERRAGAMO: sal-vah-TOR-ay fair-ah-GAH-mo

UNGARO: OON-ga-ro

VERSACE: ver-SAH-chay

YVES SAINT LAURENT: EEVES san LAWR-on

ZEGNA: ZANE-ya

Her blunt rudeness sent me into shock and then, before I could stop myself, the words poured out of my mouth. "Don't put your filthy fucking hands on that dress," I snapped, and stormed off.

That went over about as well as an editor at *Vogue* trying to get away with carrying a Marc Jacobs knockoff bag. She started hollering for the manager, who brought me over to her and tried to make me apologize to her. And maybe I would have, but she just stood there with her arms folded and a smug little smirk on her face. I looked at her and called her a stupid bitch and walked off. She started screaming in shock, but I refused to go near her again.

Somehow, I didn't lose my job. I got a really stern talking-to about how the customer is always right and I couldn't ever speak to one like that again. I got written up, but that's it. I think the manager could understand where I was coming from on that one.

Bergdorf is where I first met Robert Duffy, Marc Jacobs's long-term business partner and one of my oldest friends in New York. He still only knows me as Alex. He's always saying, "Miss J? Who?" He worked on a different floor and we would always talk together about our futures. He would lightly chastise me when I would get upset over coveting clothes my friends could afford, especially when they wouldn't let me borrow something to wear. (This displeasure was obviously compounded by the fact that I simply didn't make enough money to buy my own.) Just like when I started the paper route to buy the pair of Thom McAn shoes, he helped me realize that the only way I was ever going to get the things I wanted out of life was to go out and get them myself. He told me, "Just because they have it doesn't mean you can have it. That's theirs. Don't get upset about things that aren't yours." I thought, *Oh, right.*

I was spending so much time in the city that I finally moved out of my grandmother's place. I bounced around from one small apartment to another, sometimes even just crashing on friends' couches, until I moved into a loft on lower Seventh Avenue. It had an elevator that opened up directly into the unit (a place like that would go for millions these days, but back then, that kind of living was pretty much the norm in New York City). I shared the space with a gay couple. One worked as a doorman at a club in Chelsea, and the other was a designer who eventually developed a serious drug problem. I went through a series of different roommates over the years, but I lived longer in that place than anywhere else in NYC.

The Customer Is (Almost) Always Right

*t*he old saying is true, but don't ever feel like you need to take verbal harassment just to keep your job. Luckily a lot of companies now protect their workers from being assaulted this way by other coworkers, but if you're working at a store or a restaurant and a customer is insulting you about anything besides your work performance as it directly relates to them, I say don't take any crap. If you *can* manage to keep your tongue under wraps, try to keep calm and let your manager handle it. If you've got a cool boss, they might even ask the person to leave the store, which will not only make you feel better, it will humiliate the customer without getting you in any trouble. And it should go without saying that if you're the customer you should always treat employees with the same respect you'd want if you were in their shoes.

While I was living there, my father's health began to deteriorate fast. He had spent his entire life taking care of us and none of it taking care of himself, until he just couldn't do it anymore. He left us with just enough knowledge to become responsible adults. One winter day in December, my brothers carried this once powerful man, who was six foot two and now only weighed a hundred pounds, out of the house and into the hospital. That was the last time I saw him alive.

When I was young I thought he wasn't a very smart man, because whenever I went to him with a question, he would tell me to go look up the answer in the dictionary or at the library. I couldn't figure out how this man who could fix cars and prepare income tax returns wouldn't know the answers to simple homework questions. It wasn't until I was older that I realized he was bestowing a powerful gift on me—education. He wanted me to learn how to find things out for myself so I could learn to fend for myself out in the real world. In a way, one couldn't ask for a better father. He supported, fed, clothed, and educated all of us. He had spent his entire life teaching us how to be adults, and now that we were, he left us.

CHAPTER FOUR

THE BIG BREAK

One night I was out at Studio 54 and waltzing around in a pair of Charles Jourdan champagne heels. (Each heel looked like an upside-down champagne glass.) Back then, before Manolo and Jimmy Choo, Charles Jourdans were *the only* shoes to own, but right as I was in mid-stride, one of my heels broke. I of course recovered gracefully but it didn't go unnoticed. A woman saw what had happened and came rushing over to me. It turned out that *her* Charles Jourdan heel had just broken as well. (I know this doesn't sound good for Jourdans, but trust me, they were *it*.) I showed her how to balance on one toe so no one would see us limping around, and we became fast friends right then and there and have remained close ever since. Her name is Sharon Haver, and back then she was a stylist who did a lot of high-end catalog work and styled for the fashion section of *Star.*

We started seeing each other out more and more, and when she learned I had fashion experience beyond what she saw on the dance floor, she hired me on as her assistant. I quit Bergdorf and started working for her part-time. But I still wasn't in a place in my life where I could actually afford the clothes I wanted, so I did the next best thing—I window-shopped.

My favorite pastime back then was to get all dressed up and march the length of Madison Avenue and then back up the other side. I was my own parade, and you'd better believe I'd get stares. But I was in my own little world, stopping at the windows of every single store and boutique and studying the outfits on display, making mental notes about the stitching and the patterns and how I could replicate the cuts at home. I knew I couldn't afford anything inside these stores, so why bother going in when I could see everything I needed from the outside?

I still have a photograph of myself wearing one of the outfits I created. Brace yourselves. It was a sea-foam

one of my designs.

green wool jersey coat with a pair of homemade leg-
gings, a homemade turtleneck, and long opera gloves. I
wore them with a $25 pair of boots and a long black
scarf that hung all the way down to the back of my feet.

But even if I *had* wanted to go inside, some of the stores
wouldn't usually allow me to because of my skin color. (And
this wasn't the fifties, it was the early eighties.)

Around this time there was a rash of robberies up and down Madison Avenue. Salesgirls would open the stores in the morning, and while they were setting up, small groups of black men would run in and just grab as many items off the racks as they could and take off. This was obviously before the elaborate security systems all the stores have now.

One afternoon I was on Madison Avenue on official business. I had to return something for Sharon to a certain boutique that I will keep nameless, for soon-to-be obvious reasons. I walked up to the door, rang the buzzer, and through the glass I could see the salesgirl. She looked me up and down, folded her arms across her chest, and shouted, "We're closed."

I looked at my watch. "It's two o'clock in the afternoon," I yelled back, confused. I still remember what I was wearing—full pants with elastic in the waist, a tank top, sandals, and a full-length transparent gray light cotton linen duster coat with a lavender and white pinstripe. My hair was blow-dried straight.

"I have something to return," I stated, still confused at this point about why she wasn't letting me in. She glared at me for a few seconds more and suddenly marched off with her arms still folded. I was standing there, wondering what to do, when a young black cleaning boy appeared on the other side of the glass. "Yes?" he asked.

I couldn't believe this woman had sent a black boy to deal with the scary black (but fashionable!) man at the door. I could tell this poor kid was really embarrassed. I explained the situation, that I was there on business and I was just trying to return something for my boss. He knew I was telling the truth and got the whole mess sorted out, but it was so pathetic that this dumb shopgirl felt like she had to go and get another black guy to "translate" for her. I held it together though. Rather than being hurt by the incident, I wanted nothing more than to curse this girl out. The "take no crap" gene I'd inherited from my mother was flaring up. But unlike with the nasty old woman at Bergdorf, this time I only cursed her out in my mind instead of with my mouth.

The incident did nothing to stop me from my weekly saunter up and down Madison. Despite that one girl's ignorance, there were some salesgirls who were cool and came to recognize me because they saw me so often, looking in the window and putting on my own little runway show up and down the avenue. And this little passion of mine, this walk of inspiration and fantasy, ended up being the launching pad for my entire career. And since then Oscar winners, sports figures, and rap

Five Ways To Get Sales-people To Respect You

*P*icture this: You're on a shopping mission, have money burning a hole in your pocket, find exactly what you're looking for, and there's no salesperson in sight. (Save for one lady in the corner who's peering over like she'd rather die than waste precious words on you.) I could fully sit here and lecture shopkeepers who run their businesses poorly—after all, the customer really is always right and good service should be the staple of any fine department store or boutique—but in the interest of helping you out, here are a few tips that will help you attract the attention you might desperately need.

1. Dress well. No one will want to help you if you look like a mess. That means all your loose ends are tucked in, your hair is brushed, and you look all-around put-together. A nice bag and uns-cuffed shoes (that actually fit) help. But if you're a famous mess, then dress however you want.

2. Be polite. It doesn't behoove anyone to act

all entitled and rude. Follow the golden rule and most people will return the favor.

3. Choose your target wisely. If someone looks crazy busy and preoccupied, chances are they'll get even more flustered, if not downright angry, when you approach them. Nothing's more frustrating than being told, "Get in line!"

4. Ask questions. As a consumer and potentially paying customer, you have every right to inquire where that fabric was made or if this or that cut would look flattering on you. Engage someone by inquiring not only about the article you're interested in, but also by simply asking, "And how are *you* doing today?"

5. Butter them up. On that note, flattery will get you everywhere. If you want a salesperson's undivided attention, compliment them on what they're wearing, their hair, whatever you sincerely like about them. Then segue into what it is you need help with. You'll automatically be their new favorite customer.

6. On second thought, as a paying customer, should one kiss that much ass?

stars have all made it okay for black men and women to shop on Madison Avenue.

Not all of the shopgirls were as nasty or closed-minded as the one at that particular boutique. (Like Julia Roberts said to the shopgirl in *Pretty Woman:* "Big mistake. *Huge.*") There was a manager at Giorgio Armani named Kathyll Carnegie who always saw me stopping and looking at her windows. She loved the way I dressed and walked and would frequently come out of the store to look at the clothes with me and chitchat. We became friends over time, even exchanging numbers.

One afternoon when I stopped by she came rushing out of the store and said, "Oh my God, you have to go over to Bergdorf. I read in *The New York Times* they're doing a street casting today for a Jean Paul Gaultier fashion show at Art on the Park. I see you walking up and down the street all the time, and you've got the perfect walk."

Excited, I ran straight over to Bergdorf and there were already hundreds of people in line on the top floor, where the casting took place. Everyone had their modeling books with them, which made me nervous, but I remembered that they were casting *real* people, so I knew I had every right to be there, too. The now-famous Stephane Sednaoui was one of the assistants that day, and I had the biggest crush on him. When it finally got to be my turn he asked me to try on a pair of Gaultier pants, but I wasn't wearing any underwear. Of course I didn't let that stop me. (Sometimes I wonder if that's why I ended up booking the job.)

When they asked me to walk I went into a full-on black-girl attitude walk that I'd seen on Style with Elsa Klensch. There was a moment of silence and then someone asked me if I could try it again, only this time "be a little more normal." I took it as an insult and told them that *was* how I normally walked. But I toned it down for them. Next they snapped a few shots of me full length and profile (clothes on, of course), wrote down my size and contact information, and that was it.

Two nights later I went out to the club Limelight. I was wearing a long black crepe satin trumpet skirt, tight at the knees with a mermaid tail on it, with a blue, gold, and burnt orange bolero. I ran into a model friend of mine named Lynn who was wearing all lime green Stephen Sprouse. (*Very* chic.) As we passed each other on the steps, she said, "I saw your name on the board! You're doing the show!"

I refused to believe it until I got the actual call the next day. They were even going to pay me, $250 for two hours. Of course, I would have paid *them* to let me be in that show. It's difficult to describe the raw emotion I felt. You have to understand that at that point in my life I was

at studio 54 reopening

already staging fake runway shows in my friend Glenda's apartment. I'm not talking about trying on different outfits and strutting from one end of the room to the next; I mean full-on fashion shows, where I would pretend to be the model, makeup artist, fashion designer, show director, and audience all at once. I would yell at myself in

WALK THIS WAY:
Role-Play

*i*f someone had ever walked in on me during one of my little private runway show performances, it might have made me look like I needed to be locked up in a psycho ward for people living in alternate realities. But all that time I spent practicing, role-playing, and pretending to be in the middle of a runway show helped me prepare for the day when it finally came true. Don't ever be afraid to let yourself act out fantasies. No matter how crazy it might seem to you, let yourself get lost in your head for a while. Although I suggest doing it when your roommate/lover/parents are out of the house.

different accents, French and Italian, "Hurry, hurry, you're the next one up!" while timing myself to see how long it would take me to change into different outfits. It was pretty twisted.

Technically speaking, the Gaultier show I'd just booked wouldn't be the first time I'd appeared on a real runway. At some point in the early eighties, I attended a Claude Montana charity fashion show for the Grey Art Gallery at the Park Avenue Armory wearing a black taffeta ball gown I had made that was pulled up between my legs and pinned to the back of my waist, so that the back was still a gown but the front looked like a pair of genie pants. I wore the gown with sheer white stockings, black suede pumps with perforations and embroidery around the edges, and an off-the-shoulder black organza top with big puffed sleeves and ruffles around the top with a sash high up on the waist. This was *serious* high glamour.

Security wasn't quite as tight back then, so I was able to sneak backstage before the show began. As soon as I could tell that the models were almost ready, I decided to start the show early. I waltzed out onto the runway by myself and the crowd went into a total uproar. They were cheering and screaming as I furiously strode up and down, posing my ass off. The only thought running through my head was *Please let me get away with this.* Being hauled off by security wouldn't have been a very glamorous finale. Well, now that I think about it, maybe it would have been, but it didn't happen.

As soon as I jumped off the runway, the models

WALK THIS WAY:

If You Fall, Get Back Up

*P*ay attention, this is a metaphor for life. If you're walking down a runway and you trip and fall, and you're not really hurt, just laugh it off and keep on moving. If you lose a shoe or your heel breaks, kick it off the stage and walk on one tiptoe to keep yourself even. Or take the other one off and carry it with you. Understand? This is deep, philosophical stuff here. ◄

started walking out. It was a totally spontaneous and magic moment in fashion history.

The following week, a brief sentence appeared in a review of the show in *The Village Voice*: "At 8:15, the crowd senses the moment—a black, 6'6" drag queen in a black ruffled gown seizes the opportunity and mounts the runway in a two-minute strut. Someone yells 'Go, girl.'"

Not the thing to say to a woman in a Givenchy-inspired gown.

How To Stand Out From The Crowd

*M*y unique look is what got me started down the modeling path in Japan. Today, however, the art of being a unique individual is sadly on the decline. I see so many women blindly following trends to the point where they all look the same, and it truly breaks my heart. Back at Studio 54 and later in Japan, it was so delightful and inspiring to see people take pains to try to make themselves look special by flamboyantly expressing themselves through fashion. I'm not necessarily saying that everyone should wear completely outrageous outfits and parade up and down Madison Avenue (or Main Street, USA, for that matter), but I would encourage you to get creative when it comes to how you present yourself to the world.

Getting back to trends in general, the most important thing is to never, ever subscribe to one that isn't right for you. Example: If thigh-high boots and shoulder pads have fully come back in style, but, girl, admit it, you're really short and/or already wide in the shoulders, please step away from the craze! I don't care how hot it is. Step. Away. Additionally, I love that so many of the major designers are doing bridge lines at places like H&M and Target, but if every chick on your block is decked out in Alexander McQueen for Target, then how is it even remotely cool for you to be wearing the exact same neon pink dress? Same goes for "It" bags. Why spend a month's rent on a purse that every bland socialite on Park Avenue is trying to rock? It's so boring, and fashion is all about excitement and the unexpected! Just remember: The whatever-it-is style moment you're personally feeling, even if it seems out of bounds, could become the next big thing. Now get out there and kill it, you style arbiter, you! ◂

dare to be different.

When the morning of the Jean Paul Gaultier Art on the Park show finally arrived, I was actually very calm. To this day, that's still how I operate. I don't think about something I have to do until I'm there and it's time to do it. There's no point in getting all nervous when there's nothing you can do but wait for the moment.

The show took place down near where the World Trade Center used to stand. There was a huge runway set up and at the end of it was a rotating circle for us to stand on so the audience could get a 360-degree view of our outfits. A full gospel choir provided the music and the late, legendary Kevyn Aucoin did the makeup. The theme for the men was sort of a chimney sweep character, so many of the guys had long sideburns and all of us received smoky eyes. I couldn't help myself though—as soon as I was out of that makeup chair I went and added my own touch of frosted lips. It was my first *real* runway show, after all. Right before the show started we all lined up and Gaultier inspected each of us, saying, "Button this here, take this off, leave that on, be happy." Everything was fine with my outfit, but before I went out, Kevyn Aucoin came rushing over to me and said, "No, no frosted lips for *this* show!" He had to blot off everything I'd put on and reapply my lips. Oh well, I tried, but

WALK THIS WAY:

Take Every Opportunity

*d*espite my bravado and all my dreams, deep down inside I never really thought I was good-looking enough to be a model. But someone saw something special in me. If anyone ever offers you a job at something you never thought you'd be good at, try it out anyway. That person obviously sees a quality in you that you've somehow missed in yourself. You never know where the opportunity could take you. And if you end up hating it, you can always just quit and try something else. Like getting a job at the post office. At least you get retirement, sick leave, and vacation pay. ◢

who was I to argue with one of the world's greatest makeup artists ever?

There was one outfit change, so I got to go out on the runway twice, and just being there, in the midst of it all, was the highest high I'd ever felt. I was tall, I was thin,

photo for
paul steinitz exhibition

and I was fabulous. I walked up on that runway and walked my ass off like I had never walked before. When I reached the circular platform at the runway's end, I just posed and posed and posed.

My performance was such a success that after the show Monique Pillard, who was the president of Elite Model Management in New York at the time, came right up to me and said, "You were really great. You should do Japan." Her thinking was that the Japanese market would like me because they were more interested in the strange, weird, and bizarre, and I fit all of that. She introduced me to an agent named Hitomi Shigeta from Elite Japan who signed me up for a $20,000 contract to go and model in Japan. (Hitomi is still my agent today.) I was shocked out of my mind. It was more money than I'd ever dreamed of making at one time, and it all happened so fast. I immediately packed three huge bags of clothes and jumped on a plane.

J. Alexander

Height 187 Chest 90 Waist 72 Hips 94 Shoes 28 - 28.5 Hair Black Eyes Black

J. Alexander

Height Bust 90 Waist 72 Hips 94 Shoes 28 - 28.5 Hair Black Eyes Black

my rather versatile elite folio modeling card.

CHAPTER FIVE

A RUNWAY COACH IS BORN

Initially I was in Japan for only eight weeks, but I ended up spending the next three years of my life shuttling between there, the U.S., and Paris. My first contract required me to spend two months in Tokyo, living in an apartment in the Roppongi district. One of the first things I had to learn was how to avoid being poked in the eyes by the tops of umbrellas, because I towered over almost everyone in that city. I even had to lean down to enter my apartment because the doorway was so short, and when I took a bath, I had to fold my knees up to my chest and wash from the waist down, then the waist up. (Just like Bill Murray in that scene from *Lost in Translation*.)

Keep your boots looking new by rolling up old magazines or empty water bottles and sticking them inside. That's what keeps my brown Lu-Vus in shape!

I was fascinated by Japanese culture, especially the food—things like throwing a live fish, scales and all, into a pot of bubbling hot oil. Keep in mind I grew up with a mother from South Carolina and a dad from Virginia. I was used to fried chicken, collard greens, and baked macaroni and cheese. To add to the cholesterol-induced injury I was doing to my body, I'd smother biscuits all in butter. Up until I went to Japan, anything I ate that had a strange taste was either spit right out or seasoned with liberal amounts of salt and pepper.

Once I arrived in Tokyo though, I was constantly being invited out to dinner with clients or designers. I had to have a long conversation with myself about eating new things. I knew they were probably going to recommend things to me that I had never tried, and it would be considered incredibly rude to turn them down. My initial MO was to hold my breath while I chewed and swallowed anything I thought was going to taste strange. (Sometimes I have to do the same thing while watching a new design collection that's particularly awful.) As time went on I would accidentally get a taste of what I was eating and eventually came to enjoy the cuisine very much. I tried so many different things I never imagined putting into my mouth, like eel and roe. And believe me, Lord knows I've had some strange things in my mouth.

After booking some shows and going on a million go-sees, I came back to the States. But I got sent right back for more work. Monique had been right—the Japanese loved the outrageous outfits I created and my crazy cocktail dresses and gowns that I would wear out to parties sometimes. In a way it was like being back in New York but much easier and more fabulous—every weekend there were massive model parties and unique clubs to go to. It was different, special, and inspirational in that everyone was into dressing up wild.

I was doing so well that there was an interest from Paris, too, and the next three years were a blur of shuttling back and forth between the three cities. But after a certain amount of time had passed, I reached a conclusion that a lot of models tend to reach, which is that the novelty wears off quick. The quirky aspect of booking a man whose portfolio was made up of half-male, half-female photos was waning. The fashion world was ready for its next big thing. Instead of seeking out jobs, I just started hanging out backstage with my friends while they walked in shows. And that's how I got started doing runway coaching. I'd be lounging with friends before a show, wearing head-to-toe Versace given to me by a Saudi Arabian friend of mine named Khaled who loved to dress me. Whenever he shopped for himself he would

buy me a present—a piece here and there of the most outrageous Versace clothing he could find. I would just prance back and forth, imitating famous and not-so-famous models' walks. The girls would be screaming with laughter and shouting out the names of different models for me to imitate, and I could do each one flawlessly. I remember Oscar de la Renta coming backstage once and looking at me as if I had ten heads.

It wasn't all just silly mockery though. Sometimes a girl would be wearing a gown that was tight on the legs and had a massive train, and she'd be panicking, begging me to show her how to walk in it without falling flat on her face. And I'd be able to show her how to get down the runway, pose, turn, and walk back without tripping once. The tighter skirts require smaller steps.

The worst though was when some poor girl would come backstage after being on the runway and she would be crying because she wasn't happy with her performance. I'd tell her, "Girl, that's because you were walking like this!" and I'd imitate how she walked. "What you should have done is this," I'd say, and I'd swoop up and down the backstage area of the show.

Even though I wouldn't receive the official title until years later, the Miss J Phenomenon was born.

As I started paying even closer attention to the

shows, I noticed that there were generally forty girls in a show, and maybe twenty-five or thirty were all doing the same kind of sauntering walk, which I figured must have been the directive given by the designer. The rest of the girls would be struggling to keep up; they couldn't quite match the right walk for the show. A lot of these models were the ones who usually did editorial. They weren't used to having to walk and needed *a lot* of help. They knew how to move for a photographer but I had to show them the right kind of movement for runway. And after doing this for fun for a while, Gerald Marie (the ex-husband of Linda Evangelista and owner of Elite Paris) came up to me and said, "I see you teaching all these girls for free. You should get paid for that!"

I thought, *Really?*

In the beginning I figured it would be just a way to make ends meet. My roommate, the photographer Katerina Jebb, and I were behind on the rent on an apartment we were renting from a male model named Brad Harryman. The place we were living in was smaller than an anorexic model's pinkie finger. I used to tell my friends it was the only apartment in Paris where you could sit down, go to the bathroom, make a cup of tea, open the refrigerator, and take a shower all at once. When I could I'd sleep on friends' couches just because

---

WALK THIS WAY:

Work Spaces

*W*hen you're creative, having space to exercise that potential is very important. But it's not as important as the space in your head to work on the ideas. You don't need a huge space when you're first starting out. If you want to be a designer you might have to start out cutting fabric on a board on your bed, with a chair pulled up to it for you to sit on. You might have to move to the other side of your room to use the sewing machine. Just don't ever let a lack of space get you down. The important thing is that you are doing it. If you are living in a studio apartment, try to reserve a small corner of it to use for your

---

it was more comfortable. Since I wasn't modeling much anymore, whenever my money would run out I'd buy a cheap ticket back to New York and find some odd fashion work there, like helping stylist friends shuttle clothing. But everyone kept telling me I was never going to make any real money in Paris unless I stayed put.

endeavors. I do believe that as your space gets bigger, your creativity gets larger, but it's your soul and passion that are getting things done, not the square footage of your work area. All you really need is an electrical outlet. And some writers and artists don't even need more than a pen or paintbrush. Or you could start up any kind of business you want—say, a consulting firm for whatever you happen to be knowledgeable about—with just a desk and a phone. You don't even really need a desk; you can put your phone on your bed. Or on the damn floor. Remember that some of the richest people in America started out with tiny businesses they were operating out of college dorm rooms. Don't let constraints be your excuse. ◢

My first official runway coaching was conducted in a small apartment in the Seventh Arrondissement. It was only about ninety square feet, about the size of a Howard Johnson motel room. I'd have to have the girls walk diagonally across the room to get the longest pathway, but I didn't care. I had rented it with my hard-earned cash and it was all mine. Once things started to really take off, I was able to rent a beautiful studio space to coach out of from a photographer friend of mine named Gilles Murat in the Belleville section of Paris. It was large and during the daytime it was filled with light from its glass ceiling.

One of the hardest things about coaching full-time was figuring out what to charge. I think it's difficult for anyone to determine their own self-worth in financial terms. It was especially hard for me because I was so used to just giving away all of my information for free. My payment up until then had been the pleasure I got from watching girls find their inner confidence and end up becoming successful runway stars. I'd sit in the audience and try to communicate mentally with them, thinking, *Okay, drop the train, turn, swivel, watch the arm placement.* If they didn't do well, then I thought my job hadn't been done well.

I started out charging $100 an hour, for a minimum two-hour class. It was a number that I just pulled out of my head, based purely on what I thought I needed to make my rent and other expenses divided by how many girls I knew I had coming.

Money for clothes wasn't factored in since I still had my Saudi friend giving me gifts when he came into town. He bought so many things he later decided he didn't like

WALK THIS WAY:
Salary Wars

*S*ome people believe it's so-cially acceptable to talk openly about money when it comes to salaries. Even though I'm telling you what I initially charged, I think it is a terrible idea to talk to coworkers in an office environment about what you make. Discretion is key. You might get hurt or angry if you find out someone is making more than you, and someone else might get hurt or angry if they find out *they* are making less than you. Nobody should know how much you are making on the job except your boss. It saves everyone a lot of bad feelings, and frankly, discussing your salary at the office is just gauche. ◢

for himself that once he got home with those purchases I was usually the lucky recipient of his "old" but still totally new clothes. He loved watching me around models. In his accent he called me Grrrandma, because he thought I acted like a doting grandmother to all of the girls.

Quick side story—one evening he invited me out to a Lebanese restaurant on the outskirts of Paris, and I showed up in full drag, in a 1950s black cocktail dress that I made. No one in the restaurant was expecting it and they thought I was the entertainment for the evening. And in a way, I suppose I was.

In the end, what I was charging for the coaching was less than what most shrinks charge and I was actually providing a skill that not only boosted self-esteem but could also earn these girls money out in the real world. If a girl was really bad and just not getting it, I'd have her come back for a third class. The lesson setup went like this: For the first twenty minutes I would talk to the girl, feel her out. Sometimes I'd have two girls, and no two of the three of us spoke the same language. That's when I would turn into what I called the Big Black Vision. I would point at myself and just mime, telling them to do what I did.

In a regular class though, after we'd get done talking I'd have them show me their walks. Then we'd start with the basics, just getting them to feel comfortable in their own bodies. I'd tell them to imagine their shoulders over their hips and their hips over their heels. If you do this, you can walk elegantly without exaggeration. We'd just walk and walk and walk until they felt more comfortable and I would then point out the problems they needed to watch for. Many girls started out stiff and awkward because they were shy and uncomfortable. The hardest part was getting them to loosen up. It helped to keep the environment friendly and encouraging. The most common mistake that girls make is staring down at the runway while they walk, because that is the way they walk in real life. It's beyond me how they don't realize they need to be looking up, but old habits die harder than that horrible Uggs trend. The other big problem area is that many of them don't know what to do when they get to the end of the runway. They don't know how to make it back. Things have changed a lot since I first started teaching though. Nowadays most shows have the girls get to the end of the catwalk and turn around and come right back. But back in the day there was always a pose at the end. I'd tell my girls to hold it for three seconds.

The next day we'd go through technical aspects. This is where I would put the models in different types of clothes and teach them how to walk in each. As anyone who has ever seen an episode of *America's Next Top Model* knows, walking in a tight skirt is incredibly different from walking in a giant ball gown or a pantsuit. I'd teach them how to handle the train on a gown, how to take off a pair of gloves, and how to properly show off a handbag. I'd instruct them to pay attention to the design details on a dress, like if there was beautiful embroidered detail on the waist, they had to make sure never to put their hands on their hips in case they blocked it. I had to show them how to communicate with the outfits they were wearing. Couture walking is very different from any other kind of walking. It's much more constricted and snobbish. You have to infuse a lot of drama into both yourself and the gown in order to pull it off.

My busiest times were always about a month before the shows, which you probably know happen twice a year, for the spring and fall collections. I would have back-to-back appointments all day and sometimes I'd do evening classes. I got to be so well known that I'd be at casting calls with friends, just to hang out, and groups of girls would come parading by me, trying to show off their walk and get advice for free. I'd have to tell them that I wasn't a walking instructor after nine PM, except for certain social functions. And never on weekends. Everyone has their limits.

There was one young model who didn't get booked for a Givenchy runway show because she couldn't walk. I saw her crying in the street and she explained what had happened. I told her I could show her how, so she begged

watch and learn.

117

her agency to ask Givenchy for a second chance. She spent a day with me and got hired not only by Givenchy but also by Yves Saint Laurent, *and* landed a runway photo in the *Herald Tribune.* I was as happy as a runaway slave. Most of the girls I worked with really took the lessons to heart. They knew they'd get an ass-kickin' from me if they didn't. But there were always a few bad apples in the bunch. Some just weren't happy in front of crowds. They'd get nervous and freak out. Their agency would send them to me and they'd be begging, "Please don't make me go to the shows; I can't do them!" As if I had power over their booking schedules.

Some of these girls didn't really know how to deal with their fright. There's always champagne backstage at a show to help the girls relax and loosen up. Unfortunately, some girls can't hold their alcohol. I've seen girls throw up on clothes. But I've witnessed some crazier things backstage. I've seen girls cry over a desired dress that another girl was wearing or a dress that they'd been fitted for but was given to another girl on the day of the show. Ouch. I've seen models faint backstage, maybe from lack of eating or throwing up their food beforehand. I've seen a girl break out in hives all over her chest. She was from Albania and the poor thing was terrified—giant red blooms began appearing all over her; you could literally watch them form. I've seen girls cry because they hate the clothes they have to wear and I've even seen girls start to head out toward the runway with brown streaks on their ass because they'd eaten too many laxatives in order to stay thin. Sometimes one will freeze, like a deer in headlights, and can't make it out onto the runway when it's her turn. She'll literally have to be screamed at and pushed out onto the stage. It disrupts the flow of the entire show.

In my lessons I'd also teach the girls how to roll with the punches backstage. There's always more hectic drama than you could possibly imagine. If a designer actually asks you if you like what you're wearing, feel free to say, "If I was wearing it in real life, I'd wear it like this," if you have a different vision for the item. You never know, sometimes the designer will take out a pair of scissors and cut off whatever part of the shirt is bothering you, because he wants you to feel comfortable in what you're wearing on his runway. This is a delicate balancing act though. I don't recommend trying this unless you feel like you have a good rapport with the designer first. If you get the sense they genuinely like you, feel free to go for it. Who knows, he may end up making you his muse. But if the designer is crazy stressed and running all over the place, it's probably best to keep your opinions to yourself. I know this seems like contradictory advice, but more than just walking down a runway, I try to teach women how to gauge the runway of their lives, to look for roadblocks, to take exits and shortcuts when they appear, and most important, to pay attention to where they are going!

I always tell women *not* to try to create a signature walk. A signature walk is something that, if you end up with one, should come naturally. Sometimes they are even born out of flaws. Taking a bad walk and turning it into a good one is entirely possible. Pay attention to your flaws and make them work for you. Most people don't like what they don't understand, but my motto is: People don't buy what you're selling; you have to sell them what they don't want to buy. What I do for a living, what I teach, isn't necessarily for everyday women. But anyone can benefit from it. When you boil down the essentials, it's about walking to the rhythm of the music, walking to music that has no rhythm, and making the clothing do something that makes people say, "Wow, that's a really beautiful dress, and she looks amazing in it."

Every woman wants to feel like that. When you put on your wedding dress, you want to walk down the aisle with pride. When you go to a Christmas work party, you can make every pair of eyes fall on you if you walk in with confidence. It helps you take better photographs, too.

I raised my prices eventually, but only when my rent went up. For girls who were being sent to me by agencies, that money was coming out of their agency fee. I was meeting with enough girls at that time that I was sometimes able to pay my rent for up to three or four months in advance. I lived in terror of losing my apartment and wanted to make sure it wouldn't be yanked out from underneath me. I've moved around so much in my life and was traveling so much that it was extremely important for me to know that I had a place to come back to at night, a place I could call my own. I knew I could always finagle food or clothing if I needed it, but a roof over my head was the one thing I would always need to take care of myself.

Not long after I started officially coaching, Laila Snellman of the Paparazzi Agency, a modeling agency in Finland, heard that I had been teaching girls how to walk from one of her models, Angelika Kallio. I had shacked up with Angelika during one of my homeless model moments in Paris (my standard line for a while was, "Can I snatch a piece of your floor for a couple of nights?"). I ended up getting a gig

The Top Eight Classic Poses Of All Time

*i*t may sound like a joke straight out of *Zoolander,* but believe it or not, model agents actually encourage their girls to practice a variety of poses and faces in their mirrors at home so that when they're in front of the camera, they will naturally work what looks best on them. Even if you are not exactly the next *ANTM* candidate, chances are you will have your picture taken at some point in your life, so no matter how silly it seems, practice makes perfect! In order to get you inspired, here are the signature poses that photographers and models have developed over the years:

SPRAWLED AGAINST THE WALL—For maximum impact, the girl looks like she is absolutely *floored.* Except, like, on a wall.

THE HEAD VISE—Take one palm and press it against your face. Now take the other hand and place it on your head. Voilà! Great for close-ups.

REALLY, REALLY PO'D—Models used to be encouraged to look cheery, but in the last few decades, a sour puss rules. "Heroin chic" took this look to extremes, but at its basic level, looking like you have PMS and you'll bite someone's head off if they even get near you should suffice.

GLAMOUR SMOKING—There is absolutely nothing glamorous about lung cancer, but this shot continues to be iconic (although increasingly less so). Good riddance!

ARE YOU THERE, GOD? IT'S ME, MODEL—This entails a beatific, otherworldly stare into the great beyond. Deep, very deep.

ALL HIPS, ALL THE TIME—Celebs have totally copied this look for the red carpet: Standing, cross one leg in front of the other and jut your hip forward. Works like a charm.

"WHO, ME?!"—You look surprised! Your hands are pressed to your chest! Your mouth is wide open! You look crazy!

THE JUMP—This is the mother of poses, which entails a model simply leaping into the air. She can look jubilant or dour, depending on the mood and the photographer's disposition. ◢

in Finland to teach Finnish girls how to walk for Finnish Fashion Week. It would have been a great experience, except for one horrible thing that happened to me there.

Finland has changed a lot, but when I first arrived there almost fifteen years ago, it could be rough for a black gay man. One time I was sitting in a café minding my own business when a drunk man at a nearby table suddenly began harassing me. He yelled out that I was a nigger. He said I had brought AIDS to their country. He looked at me with sheer disgust, and I was shocked. I ignored him and just held my head high, but the next day I was walking down the street with a tall blond model I had been working with when out of nowhere another drunk man came up and tried to kick me in the crotch. It was a horrible moment. I think he thought I was in the country stealing his women. (Little did he know I was there stealing their men!) I think I was considered just a big ol' black threat. There are certain things I don't let bother me, and that was one of those things. When he tried to kick me he could barely stand on his own because he was so wasted, and he fell on the street in the ice. My first reaction was to stomp him—not kick him, but to stomp him in his face while he was on the ground. It was my very first reaction, but even quicker, I had to think not to do it. It was my true South Bronx ghetto upbringing. *Mother******, you tried to kick me, I'll kick your ass back,* was what I was thinking.

But then I realized, *He's drunk, he's stupid, and he's mad.* I was able, once again, to calm myself down and just continue on my way.

Soon after I returned from Finland, the same client took me to Sweden's Fashion Week for the same reason and I started traveling twice a year to both locations on a regular basis. Elite eventually took me on full-time, too. So I started working for the Elite Model Look, their international competition where they scout different countries and modeling agencies for new girls to hire. Every year there is a huge competition from country to country, ending with a giant Elite contract. I was being sent to London, Slovakia, the Czech Republic, and Korea to teach the girls how to walk before the big main event. The shows were fun but they were usually a big mess— I'd be working with anywhere from fourteen to twenty girls, only around half of whom spoke English, and the rehearsals always started late because of confusion and disorganization. For all of these shows, local choreographers were brought on to work as well, and it was difficult to try to marry my walking skills with the choreographers' moves. There was more than one personality clash during those times.

WALK THIS WAY:

Breathe First

*I*t's so easy to spontaneously react when someone calls you a name or threatens some sort of violence. That first gut reaction to someone else's nastiness is one of the reasons why our jails and prisons are so full. People are so hot-headed that they attack when they're attacked. I know I said earlier to stick up for yourself and fight back, but I mean that more for scenarios where someone is trying to keep you down. When you're faced with someone who is drunk or possibly dangerous, you need to breathe deep, ignore them, and continue on your way. Especially if the person is drunk and threatening physical violence. It's a constant struggle for me. On the one hand, I have my South Bronx upbringing that tells me to kick the ass of anyone who is messing with me, but I also try to sense how much of a threat the person really is. If a stranger is screaming hysterically at you, just take a breath and try to move on rather than egg them on. If someone is coming after you and trying to attack, run and get to a crowded place. I can't stress this enough: choose your battles in life.

After I started working heavily overseas I began to branch out into getting directly involved with the casting and production of shows. It was a new and different kind of project but one I really wanted to gain more experience in. It's important to always branch out of your comfort zone. I was so used to just teaching models how to walk that actually creating an image for a designer through casting the girls was a little bit nerve-racking for me. You want to have the *right* girl. I think normally what someone would have done in my situation is find all the hottest girls and book them, to please the designer. But I wanted to try something new and different. I looked at all the girls on the B list, because I knew how badly they would want the opportunity to get cast in a great show and that they would probably work extra hard to make a good impression. I decided to take a risk. I'd book thirty total. I'd have the designer's favorite twenty models, five B-list girls, and five that nobody had *ever* heard anything about. I wanted to keep it fresh, keep it moving, and maybe even create a star. I knew that the show wasn't mine, that I was work for hire, so I was taking a gamble. For one Bill Blass show designed by Lars Nilsson, I wanted to use five black girls to open the show, and the company had never done anything like that before, at least to my knowledge. I told the team it

WALK THIS WAY:

Don't Go To A Pizza Parlor To Get A Tuna Fish Sandwich

*E*ven though my career was really taking off at this point, I was honestly just happy to be paying the rent. It wasn't an accident though, that I was able to do so in the field that I loved. If you want to be in fashion, you place yourself in fashion wherever possible. It could be a department store, backstage at a fashion show, assisting a stylist, whatever. Do whatever comes your way in the field you love, no matter how menial it may seem. Place your-

would be really great, but they were very reluctant at first. But I convinced them to use the girls and in the end, everybody loved it. European designers had been booking multiple black models in their shows for years and it was no big deal, but Bill Blass was considered very Park Avenue.

I wasn't trying to rebel against any fashion standard, I

self within it and keep your eyes and ears open for opportunities. Some people don't know how to take advantage of their surroundings because they are too busy with only trying to get ahead. You know how Tyra is always telling models, "Smile with your eyes"? Well, you've got to learn to *listen* with your eyes as well. Paying attention to what's going on around you will help you get ahead, but it's not all about hearing about other jobs. You've got to keep your eyes open and *see* where people need help, even if they don't realize it, and then offer up your services. This goes for any type of job or career you are seeking out. ◄

just wanted to point out that when you ask me to get involved with your show, you're asking for my opinion, guidance, and third eye. With the Bill Blass show I took a risk and it paid off. I believed in the project, and I believed in what the creative director, Lars, was doing, because I love his clothes.

I wasn't earning play money at the time. I was work-

*lars and i backstage
at the bill blass show*

ing to pay the rent, to make sure no one ever showed up at my doorstep and said I was getting evicted or my electricity was about to be turned off. Besides my Versace pieces, I was still dressing in hand-me-downs that I would alter and spice up to create one-of-a-kind pieces.

One day I was approached during a fitting at the Ritz by a man named Carlos DeSouza, who worked for Valentino. He asked if I would be willing to work with a Dutch model who couldn't walk and to contact her agency. It was surreal to be hired by a company owned

WALK THIS WAY:

Get Out Of Your Comfort Zone

*t*he best way to know if you're on the right track in life is if you find yourself doing something that you are terrified of failing at. It means that you're willing to take the steps and make the sacrifices necessary to get to where you want in life. I've taught models who were terrified of being in front of a crowd of people on a runway. It was fine for them to perform in front of a camera and a small crew, but the thought of a giant room full of eyes sent them into a full-on hissy fit. It was the ones who faced that fear and kept walking forward, taking advice, and really applying it to themselves who went on to have major careers. So remember, fear can be your friend, not something to run away from.

by the man who once partied at Studio 54 at the same time I was taking my first elegant baby drag steps there.

Because of that, it felt good to help out models taking their own baby steps out into the world. Sometimes I encountered a lot of teenage models who had been removed from their homes at a very early age. There's been a huge influx of girls from the Eastern bloc countries over the years, and many of them are so young that they haven't even learned proper grooming techniques yet. They're beauties but don't realize they need to start shaving. Some of them don't even know how to use a tampon. I became a sort of mentor for a lot of these girls. Their beauty was an incredible paycheck for the family, and when you're poor, you're very quick to accept any job that helps you make money even if it means leaving home at the onset of puberty. All of these girls worked hard. Most of them were very smart and always did what they were told. It isn't as harsh as it sounds though. The agents make sure the parents are aware of everything that is going on and let them spend a week with their daughter, so they can walk around with them on go-sees and see how the whole industry works. I think that's very important, because it was usually the girls who had parents who watched over them who got ahead. Sometimes the parents who watch over them can be pretty scary though—during one model competition in Beirut, I got stuck riding in an elevator with the father of a girl who hadn't made the finals. He was glowering so intensely at me that I wasn't sure I was going to make it out of there alive.

Besides the money, I was living off of the excitement of watching all the girls I taught do well. But the excellent side benefit was the access I gained to the kings and queens of fashion. I got to meet Alexander McQueen through Katy England, his right hand, at his workspace in London while I was working with a black model named Aischa. I adored Alexander. I had read so much about him and watched him any time he was on television. I was happy to learn that in person he was quite hilarious. But he was also so talented and ahead of his time. He likes the new, in the same way that Karl Lagerfeld does. While Alexander was designing for Givenchy in Paris, he ended up sending one of his girls over to me with a dress and a pair of heels she was supposed to wear in his show. I studied it and perfected a walk for her that would help the dress flow. Model agencies weren't the only ones looking to me for help anymore; my skills were now known among the fashion world's most elite.

Karl Lagerfeld

*M*adonna may have reinvention covered on the pop music front, but if there's a single designer out there who knows how to stay relevant, it's undoubtedly the irrepressible Karl Lagerfeld, who can teach us all a thing or two about keeping up appearances. Even though he's had a long, illustrious career—after emigrating from Germany to Paris in 1953, he worked as an illustrator and designed for Balmain, Jean Patou, Repetto, Chloé, Fendi, and Tiziani (watch the movie *Boom,* with Elizabeth Taylor and Richard Burton, to see some of the clothes Karl designed when he was at Tiziani; my friend André Leon Talley made me watch it with him late one night and the clothes are beyond), before rising to more widespread prominence as the visionary behind today's Chanel.

Unlike some old-school designers, Karl Lagerfeld never gets tired or boring. Maybe it's because he's never afraid to try new things. He was one of the first designers to collaborate on a more affordable line with H&M (before that, major houses were hesitant because they thought going mainstream would "taint" their prestige factor), and now *everybody's* clamoring to do it. His artistic forays into fashion photography have been hugely successful, as has his costume design career and his development of an eponymous line, K Karl Lagerfeld. He's fascinated by music and literally owns hundreds of iPods, which he stashes around his various homes, and he's the first one to embrace a hot new model, artist, musician, or starlet. By consistently staying ahead of other designers and making great strides to keep up with pop culture, art, and fashion trends, Lagerfeld is truly the embodiment of agelessness.

CHAPTER SIX

AMERICA'S NEXT TOP MODEL: THE BEGINNING

I first met Tyra Banks backstage at a show. We said our casual hellos and then started seeing each other at different runway presentations. She was living in Paris and we soon became close friends, but she never really liked living in Paris (maybe she'll tell you about that in *her* memoirs one day). After she moved back to America we stayed in touch over the phone and we'd have hour-long conversations, catching up on all the Parisian fashion gossip. But I never in a million years dreamed that we would end up working together the way we do now.

I was the first person that Tyra approached about being on *America's Next Top Model*. Well, actually she

137

wasn't the first person to talk to me about appearing on *America's Next Top Model.* It was her mother. I was still working for Lars at Bill Blass at the time, and we had just finished a show. I remotely checked my answering machine in Paris, and there was a call from Tyra's mother that said, "Hi, J., this is Momma Carolyn calling. How are things, how are you? Listen, Tyra's developing a show, I think you'll be perfect for it, so call us back and let us know who we talk to in order to get you on it." They had no idea I was working in New York at the time, so I called her back. The conversation went as follows:

"Hey, Momma. What's going on, girl?"

"J. Alexander, I'm so glad you called me back."

I could hear Tyra in the background going, "Hi, J.!"

I said, "What's going on?"

Her mother handed the phone to Tyra, who was so excited as she explained the show's concept to me. She was going to approach the networks with the idea of a reality show where every week a girl is kicked off after trying to complete modeling tasks like the ones Tyra had gone through during her career, things like having to wear bathing suits in freezing cold weather and modeling winter coats in the Sahara desert. But she wanted to teach them real technical skills, too, and that was where I came in, as the show's runway coach.

*hanging with momma
carolyn in los angeles.*

"When are you going to be in New York?" she asked.

She was thrilled to learn that I was already in New York, so I just walked up to her hotel at Sixty-third Street and Madison. We sat down and we talked out all the different show concepts, and that was it. I wanted in; it sounded fun. About a week later I ended up on a conference call with the producers. I can't stand being on conference calls. I'm always afraid that I'll be on speakerphone and not know who's in the room, and accidentally say something that might hurt that person's feelings.

Whenever I have to be on a conference call I warn people up front about that and tell them that they are responsible for any wounded egos, not me.

I explained to everyone on the call how I usually work with girls, that it's no more than four girls at a time for a two-hour class. I knew nothing about television, but I'd been doing coaching for such a long time at that point that I figured I'd just do my thing. You got what you got with me, and then we were done. Sort of like the best one-night stand of your life. Turns out that was *so* not the case.

The very first episode I shot was in Brooklyn and I brought all my props, like different types of clothes and accessories to model. They started filming and I immediately hated it. I was still operating under the assumption that shooting a television reality show was like shooting a documentary, so I just did what I normally do—which is teach. But the producer kept saying, "Stop, wait, let's try it this way." Or, "Cut, let's do a different take." There were moments when I would be talking to the girls, trying to get them to rest because they were exhausted or trying to get to know them a little better so I could see where I could push them and what their different strengths and weaknesses were. But the producer didn't want me to do any of that and he was constantly telling me to stop what I was doing and saying, "Just do it this way; this is what I need."

I finally got fed up and stormed off the set, telling them that was *not* how I worked. In retrospect, it's hilarious. I was so inexperienced in the ways of television. I was in the midst of getting my reality TV cherry popped. I was demanding to work as if it was a normal two-hour class—coaching the models, taking breaks, making sure they were resting their feet, joking with them, as if the producers possibly had time for all of that. Boy, was I off target.

My other big issue initially was that I had a real problem with writers from the show trying to write lines for me. On that first cycle I was asked to say things like "This girl is here because of such-and-such and it's fiiiieeeerce!" (Damn. Does it count if I use the F-word if I'm quoting someone else?) It was so obvious to me that there was some heterosexual man stuck in a writing room trying to write the way he thought gay men in the fashion world talked. I had the same problem when I worked for E!'s *Fashion Police.* They'd want me to say things like "Oooh, child, girl! Nuh-uh, honey child! Oooh, that's *faaaaabulous.*" Let me make this perfectly clear. I. AM. NOT. THAT. GIRL. Caroline Pedrix, one of my former modeling bookers and a dear friend, used to

WALK THIS WAY:

Public Speaking

*e*veryone will have to give a speech at some point in their life, whether it's at a wedding or addressing your entire company at the executive retreat. I've found that the best way to handle public speaking, especially if you are nervous, is to write everything you want to say ahead of time, and then distill it all down to a small number of talking points. Once you know your main subjects, just memorize those in order and ad lib the rest. It's easier than memorizing an entire speech. If you're really nervous then write down a few bullet points under each subject on three-by-five-inch index cards so you can refer to them. Practice in front of a mirror beforehand, and then practice in front of some friends and family so you get used to an audience. If you have the right equipment, videotape yourself and analyze your strengths and weaknesses. If you have a job that requires you to do a lot of presenting and public speaking and you're a naturally shy person, take a public speaking course. Most local community colleges offer them, as do private companies. Trust me, it's well worth the money. And the most important thing is to *know your subject.* I once had to do a speech at a party for an *America's Next Top Model* special that was debuting on the Oxygen network. I got up there in front of all the guests and Oxygen executives and went on and on about what a great network it was and how much I loved their show *Bridezillas.* It turns out that show is on the Women's Entertainment network. Oops.

Since Jay Manuel and I do so much public speaking together, he's also given me some helpful advice. He says to always remember the Three Ws—the Where, What, and Why. If you can remember those three details about whatever it is you're speaking about, then you're golden.

tell clients, "Trust me, you'll get your money's worth. With J. Alexander, what you see is what you get and a whole lot more. Fo' sho." I understand how it's easy to fit me into a box or a category of person, but watch me on television a little bit closer next time. I'm actually rather reserved, and my delivery is usually quite deadpan.

The producers finally got what they needed from me after shooting the first cycle, but I vowed that I would never do that again. Then seven months later I got a phone call that they wanted me to come back. I'd already told my television agent, Alex Schwab, that I'd stick needles in my eyes before that happened because I felt that what they were doing wasn't high fashion. And when I told that to the producers as they were trying to get me back, they said, "You're exactly right, big man, it's television."

It was like a little lightbulb went off in my head. I just got it. Well, that and a substantial raise. None of us involved ever thought the show would have the staying power that it does. We figured maybe four cycles at the absolute most. At the time I'm writing this, I'm about to start shooting cycle *thirteen*.

Many people don't realize that I haven't always been Miss J. For most of my career I was known as J. or Alex. It wasn't until the first season of the show that one of the

WALK THIS WAY:
Don't Resist Authority

*N*o matter how much you hate your boss, you have to respect him or her. There is an automatic response in many people to buck against authority. For me, strong authority figures always make me think of my mother and my earlier desperate desire to rebel against her and escape my old life. In a career environment, you can't do that. You have to respect your elders, because even if someone is the nastiest, meanest witch you've ever met, they're still the person who has the power to shift your life in different directions—or worse, slow the process if they don't like you either. Any time I was working with a new designer's models for a show and I didn't agree with the direction he was going in, I would always concede and say, "It's your show, and I'm happy to be working with you on it." If I make suggestions and the designer doesn't like them, I don't let myself get hurt or upset. Maybe I'm a little annoyed, but ultimately I need their good recommendation more than I need to hear a different style of music for the girls to walk to. And at the end of the day, I have the satisfaction of at least knowing that I spoke my mind. ⚜

contestants, Robin, called me Miss J because she couldn't differentiate between Jay Manuel and me during her critique. Tyra asked her which Jay she was talking about and she blurted out "Miss J." Tyra loved it and decided that the name should stick. And stick it did, although personally I think Jay Manuel is more "Miss J" than me. (Just kidding, Jay!)

When the show first started airing, I was used to being recognized here and there. People in the fashion industry knew me from the runway shows, and every now and then a stranger would recognize and approach

the two j's.

me because I filmed segments for a few shows, like *Good Morning America* and *Nightline,* in Paris. I'd usually be a small part of a larger fashion story, in which I'd get introduced and they'd tell a little story about me being a young boy from the Bronx who teaches models how to walk. I'd also done some magazine and newspaper interviews.

But everything preceding the show pales next to my newfound exposure. *America's Next Top Model* ended up bringing millions of people who watched the show into my life and were somehow discovering every place that I ate breakfast, lunch, and dinner.

The first major crazy moment of being recognized by a mob of people came when Russell Simmons asked me to speak at the High School of Fashion Industries on their career day. All of the students gathered in the auditorium from eight AM until noon listening to different people from the fashion industry talk about their jobs, so the kids could get an idea of what sorts of careers were available for them when they graduated. I was there on behalf of Baby Phat, since I had worked on some of their shows. We were one of the last segments, so I arrived late, via taxi. I went in through a back door and was put in a tiny little broom closet of a room to wait until it was my turn to go out and talk. There were more than sixteen hundred students and faculty in the auditorium, getting restless after a day of presentations. Right before I came on they were showing a video of a Baby Phat fashion show, and the kids were really into it, since the label celebrates hip-hop and glam for an inexpensive price. Nobody could have anticipated what came next. A woman from Russell's production company announced that they had a special guest. I started to walk out onstage just as she said, "Please welcome, from *America's Next Top Model*—" and before she could even finish the sentence the audience screamed, *"MISS JAAAAYYYYY!!"*

My body actually kind of shuddered, and I couldn't get any words out of my mouth. I stood there in shock, with my lips opening and closing like a fish, with no sound coming out. Some kids even tried to rush the stage and the teachers were in an uproar, trying to get everyone to calm down. The whole time I kept thinking, *Me? They're doing this for me?*

I wasn't sure what to do, so when I finally found my voice, I said, "Who wants to be America's next top model?" and the screaming started all over again. Everyone started chanting, "Walk, walk, walk!"

I said, "I'm not going to walk, I'm going to talk."

"Talk, talk, talk!" they chanted back at me. Despite

being thoroughly freaked out, I had to give it up to them for their enthusiasm.

I talked to them about the importance of staying in school and how even if they hated it, they should find at least one subject that they could get excited about, and that they'd be surprised how much of the retained information would come in handy later in life. I told them that I remembered how high school felt like a waste of time, but if you can just get through it, having that diploma opens up the next set of doors for you. The most important thing is to make sure that you don't stagnate.

I love having fans and really appreciate how sweet so many of them can be. But unfortunately there are always going to be people in life who don't like you, no matter how nice you are to them. For whatever reason, people make up preconceived ideas about total strangers, and when that happens, the only thing you can do is ignore them and hold your head high and keep it moving. During one fashion week in New York, I showed up at a runway presentation by a designer. I had brought a director, Leola Westbrook, as my date and she was interested in possibly calling in one of the designer's dresses to wear to the Emmys. When we arrived at the door, a very tall guy in black with long hair took one look at me and said, "I'm sorry to do this to you, but I've been told they really don't want you here." I was stunned and totally caught off guard. Now, normally I would have given that person a sweet smile, but the words that came out would have been so damn razor sharp. Where I spit, no grass grows. But I was so embarrassed since I had brought the director with me that I just gave the gatekeeper my seat assignment and walked away. I felt terrible that I had brought this director friend of mine after speaking so highly about the designer.

Two days later I was invited to G-Star's fashion show, where Leola and I did the whole red carpet thing and sat in the front row. I got in the car they sent for me and headed to the after-party. Lo and behold, the same tall guy was working the door and telling people that the fire department wasn't letting anyone else in. I called a friend who was working inside, and he let me in through a back door. As Leola and I were leaving the party, she noticed the same tall guy from the front door talking to someone. As I continued to walk out she stopped and asked him what had happened the other night. He explained that he had gotten explicit directions from his bosses at the PR firm he worked for that I wasn't to be let in. He told Leola that he had a lot of respect for me because I had been so gracious about it, and he was clearly embarrassed that he had been put in that position.

I still don't know why I was shut out of that show. I can only assume it was because the people at this particular public relations firm had probably only ever really gotten to know me from *America's Next Top Model* and not as a legitimate long-standing member of the fashion community. Which means they hadn't been doing their homework. I have fun with *ANTM*, and I know I look like a clown and a fool sometimes, but it's just part of the game. Some people think I'm the ugliest thing on TV, that I'm a mess, that I want to be a woman. They're confused by the fact that I'm called Miss J. But no one can deny that I know what I'm talking about when it comes to walking on a runway. Someone may not like the TV show that I'm on, but that show does have power. I have a larger voice because of it. And as fate would have it, the same designer later begged the producers of *ANTM* for two weeks to do our final runway show for cycle twelve with them in Brazil. All I have to say about that is God don't like ugly, and Rosa Chá was such a better choice and a total dream to work with.

Sometimes I watch people walking down the street, and I think, *Are they people I'd want to know? What are they like at home? What do they do for fun? How much*

WALK THIS WAY:

You Never Know Who Someone Will End Up Being

*B*esides just practicing basic human kindness, the other reason to be nice to everyone you meet is that you never know who they will end up being. If you bitch out some shopgirl who just rang something up incorrectly, then watch out, because she just might end up being your boss somewhere down the line—or a designer whose runway show you're dying to get into. The person who you just cut in front of in line could be the head of the company whose business you're trying to win. If it's hard for you to just be naturally nice to people, think of it in terms of what it might get you—or prevent you from doing—in the future. ◢

money do they make? Is that man cheating on his wife?
These are the things I think about just to pass the time
and amuse myself. But I would never take my thoughts
about a stranger and apply them to reality. For someone
to judge me based solely on what they see on television
or in the streets alone is hurtful, not to mention rude
and small-minded. And unfortunately the world is full of
people like that. The only thing to do is hold your head
up high and keep on believing in yourself. In most situations, if someone snaps at me, I snap back. When you're
nasty to me, I get nasty, too. But if I see someone who is
in a position to be nasty and I know where it's coming
from, I don't respond back that way. I just keep neutral.
If you try to come at me from a position of power, I'll respond differently, because I know you're someone who
needs to be handled differently. Since I am also in a position of power sometimes, I don't mind exacting a little
professional revenge. That PR firm has lost hundreds of
thousands of dollars of business so far because they are
no longer on my list of people I recommend to directors,
producers, and stylists. (It's all about karma, and sometimes you have to give karma a little kick in the butt.) In
my case, people who aren't fans of the show who judge
me just because I'm on it are screwed. What they don't
realize is that all the celebrities they are so desperately

trying to get into the front row are people I've either worked with or who are fans of my verbal honesty, and I've even had dinner at their homes.

Truth be told, I actually don't even watch *America's Next Top Model* anymore. Not because I don't want to, but because I don't have the time, what with always flying all over the world. I usually try to catch clips of the show on YouTube, and I almost always forget what I said during filming until I see it again on-screen. Lest you worry about it, I can confirm that the judging panel is a true democracy. All of our votes count. Sometimes even Tyra gets voted down. Many times I get voted down, too. I'm not going to give away any secrets of the show, because that isn't what this book is about. But I will tell you this much—there are two *ANTM* winners who I didn't think deserved it. I didn't think they were the nicest and warmest of people, and it seemed like they were just faking their way through how they *thought* a top model should act. Uh-oh, I hope I didn't just start a scandal!

WALK THIS WAY:

Analyze, Don't Criticize

*a*nother important thing that my mother taught me to do is think critically when you're up against something or someone that you can't quite understand. Here's a hypothetical scenario: Say I was walking down the street with my mother when I was a child and I called someone ugly because they had a large birthmark on their face. Her line of reasoning would go like this: she'd ask, "Why did you call him ugly?" My response would be, "Because he has a big scary thing on his face." Her response would be, "Does that really change anything about him?" It sounds simple, but too often people forget this—just because someone *seems* different, be they transgender, overweight, or even gay, it doesn't mean that they *are* any different than anyone else in this world. They eat, sleep, and shit just like everyone does. I try to live my life by this lesson. And if someone is in a place where they are less enlightened than you and are calling someone else names, then before you just attack them, try to step back and take a look at how they arrived at that ignorant place to begin with. Then try to educate or guide them into a better position. ◄

CHAPTER SEVEN

YOU GOTTA WORK.
NO, SERIOUSLY.

A while back I was working on a big fashion show with my friend Kimora Lee Simmons. Now, I adore Kimora, but she has a problem with technology addiction. There isn't a moment in the day where she doesn't have a BlackBerry, a second cell phone, and a laptop engaging her attention three different ways.

In addition to all those machines Kimora is attached to, she also had three different assistants constantly scurrying around her. There were so many nights where I'd be standing as close as I could to her with Polaroid pictures of the hair and makeup tests in one hand and model composites in the other. I'd need her to approve

157

Sugar mixed with baby oil makes a great homemade skin scrub. If you don't like sweet scents, use oatmeal and olive oil to slough off your dead skin.

Talk To A Person, Not A Machine

*W*e've become a spoiled world as far as communication goes. Computers do all of our talking for us. Computers spell for us, cell phones send letters for us, and you don't even have to use that same cell phone for talking. You can just text. We've become lazy with a lot of things that we should really be taking care of ourselves. You can call me a Luddite, but I'd rather talk to a person about my money instead of a machine. I always go to a bank teller to deposit or take out money. Not only does it reassure me that my cash is being handled correctly, but it keeps me connected to the human world. If you don't have time for that then at least try to get a real voice on the line when you call somewhere and you have to go through an automated menu. I've found that just pressing zero or saying "operator" usually gets me connected to a live person. ⚒

them so I could tell the rest of the staff to go home to their families, but I couldn't even get near her desk. One night I arrived with all my paperwork for her to approve and ended up standing there for twenty-five minutes while she multitasked on two different devices and typed on another. I finally got so sick of waiting that I yelled, "*Focus!* Look at these and tell me which ones you want to use! I need only five minutes of your time and I've been waiting here for almost half an hour." And she made her choices and some corrections right then and there. The next time she was trying to do five things at once and not paying attention to me, I gave her a pinch on the arm.

"Ouch!" she yelled. "Don't do that; I'm not your child!"

"Sometimes you act like one," I said. "And right now you need to pay attention to me. Who do you like on this board?" Once I was able to get her to focus on me and me alone, I felt better about the job I was doing. There are so many mistakes that can be made in any job, and getting someone to pay attention makes it so much easier. In my case with Kimora, I needed her to look closely at all the girls I had booked to make sure there weren't any that she didn't like. When I have a designer's or casting director's undivided attention, I can fight for the creative team that I think are the best people to help get the designer's vision on the runway. I'll explain that I think a certain makeup artist is great, or in Kimora's case, that I didn't want girls who were too thin, because thin girls don't look too good in Kimora's clothes; you need to have a body to rock her looks. The point is to always try to get your boss to hear what you need to say, because you don't want to be the one responsible if he or she is unhappy in the end.

backstage at bill blass with kimora.

> WALK THIS WAY:
> ## It's Okay To Say No
> *W*hile it's always good to say yes to extra work if your boss gives it to you, in other arenas of your life it's sometimes good to tell people no. If you're a people pleaser, then you are probably wearing yourself too thin. Take care of yourself first, even if it means, say, having to tell your best friend that you can't babysit or telling your boss that you can't make it to that weekend work retreat. If you need to spend time in a hot bath in order to keep yourself from snapping, then do it. ◢

I know there's a million-dollar business built on teaching people how to multitask, but I just don't believe in it. I don't think that things get done properly when you try to do too much. It's harder to focus and mistakes will happen. It's far better to concentrate on one task at a time. This applies to your interactions with others, too. I don't recommend going around pinching people like I

WALK THIS WAY:

Job Interviews

*t*he most important words to remember in a job interview are *please* and *thank you*. It's good to come across as self-assured, but you need to leave your cocky attitude at the door. You don't have to worry about wearing the most expensive clothes, but make sure you look clean and neat and put together and that you are wearing the appropriate clothes for the job you are interviewing for. You might want to cover up the tattoo on your arm if you're applying for a corporate position, but if you're applying for a job in a creative field, then by all means let it show. And be sure to wash and iron or press whatever you are going to wear.

did, but if your boss is on the phone and you need to hand her a document, wait until she's off the phone and done multitasking before handing it to her, because otherwise there's a chance she'll just put the paper on her

Job interviews are not the place to sit and sulk in a chair and act like the world owes you everything. Be responsive, polite, eager, and pleasant. I know this sounds like the most obvious advice in the world, but you'd be shocked at how many people out there don't follow these easy rules when looking for work. *Especially* in the fashion and modeling industries. There are enough bitches in the fashion industry already and no one wants to hire another one. Just because it's a business that celebrates attitude doesn't mean you should put one on when trying to enter the field. As my grandmother said on her deathbed, "Have manners and respect for people, because respect and manners will carry you where money will not."

desk and it will quickly get lost in the pile. Then what are you going to do, blame her because she wasn't paying attention when you handed it to her?

Keep a to-do list if you need to, and give every task

your full attention. I feel like I learn so many things every single day, it's hard to keep it all in my head. I've always wanted to keep a journal, but I just never seem to have the time to do it. But I'm going to give this to you as advice anyway. Keeping a journal is a fantastic way to look back on your day, your week, the whole month. Even if you just have something simple like a school notebook that you keep by your bed, it's healthy to write down one new thing you learned that day before you go to sleep. I do this in my head at night, but I always wish that I'd started writing everything down years ago. (For one thing, it would have made writing this book a lot easier!) Think of it as part of your daily exercise routine, except you are exercising your mind instead of your body.

CHAPTER EIGHT

DADDY J.

I have a five-year-old godson in Arcachon, France, named Arthur, whose mother, Marie O'Neill, is one of my best friends. Not long ago, Arthur asked me, "Uncle J, how did you have a baby?"

I wanted to answer him honestly, so I said, "Me and my ex-boyfriend put both of our special baby-making juice in a tube, and the mother put it between her legs and squirted it inside her."

"That's disgusting," he said.

"Why?" I asked.

"Because you aren't married!" he answered exasperatedly.

Taking two antacids before bed each night can help balance out acids in your skin and help clear breakouts. Plus, every woman can use the extra calcium.

He didn't care at all that I was gay or even really comprehend the logistics of what I had just told him. He just thought only married people should have babies. Obviously he is wrong, and we're all making sure to teach him that now.

So, how many of you were shocked just now to learn that I have a child of my own? I purposely wanted to casually mention that fact initially because really, you shouldn't be shocked. Many men my age have children. There's nothing strange about it. Our method may seem a little unconventional, but these days, it really isn't. My son's name is Boris. His mother is a French lesbian and his biological father is an ex-boyfriend of mine, a doctor named Alex. We are all actively involved in rearing Boris, and the experience has enriched my life beyond imagination. His mother tried three different times to become pregnant, but it didn't happen until the third attempt. Alex and I wanted there to be a chance that the child could be either of ours, hence the shared baby batter. When Boris finally arrived, he came out quite white, very Slovak and Eastern European looking. I turned to Alex and said, "Whoops, he's yours."

To borrow from the title of an insipid American television show, kids say the darnedest things. When Boris was around three and a half, I was over at "Dr. Alex's"

holding little boris.

house with him (I'm Big Alex) and he was watching television while eating a snack. I asked him in French if he was done eating, and he turned to me and said, "Silence, African! I am looking at the television."

I was laughing my butt off inside. "Excuse me?" I asked.

He repeated, "African!"

"I'm American," I said, while trying not to laugh.

He did this three different times.

I let it slide, but his father, Dr. Alex, confronted him about it, asking why he had said that Big Alex was African. "Because," he answered, as honestly and simply as possible, "all the people I see in the street who are that color are African." Dr. Alex had to explain to him that there were black Americans, black Caribbeans, a whole assortment of people in this world. And Boris immediately understood. He's an incredibly smart child. He was toilet trained at a year and three months. He refuses to drink out of plastic and will use only glass. He insists on wearing nice shoes. I think somehow my fashion genes must have slipped in there.

I firmly believe that if your child is speaking to you like an adult, then you should answer him like an adult. When Arthur wanted to know how I had a baby, there was no reason in my mind to make up some story about a stork. You need to listen to children when they speak to you and ask questions because you will usually end up learning some sort of lesson yourself if you answer them truthfully.

If you have kids of your own or are even just babysitting, you should always give children boundaries and let them know that there are repercussions when they push those boundaries. But keep in mind it's okay to let them

WALK THIS WAY:

Be Aware Of Your Effect On Other People

*i*t's easy to forget that while you are just going about your day-to-day life, you are affecting other people with each word you're saying. Watch what comes out of your mouth, because even a casual joke can come across as cruel to someone else. I know I can be quite intimidating when I enter a room, so I always make sure to say a nice hello around people I don't know well at first. I don't want to start running my mouth off and fooling around in case I accidentally hurt someone's feelings. I always hated it when someone looked down on me (not *physically* looked; that's rare) so I make sure to try never to do it to someone else. If you are in a position of power, don't ever misuse it. You never know when you're going to get knocked off that pedestal. ◄

push every now and then if they try to, because that way you'll know they will push themselves further in their career and their life when they're older when it comes to new opportunities. I've always believed that "No" isn't reason enough. If I tell Arthur or Boris, "No," I will explain *why* I'm telling them "No." Hopefully this won't bring on Child Protective Services, but I'm the type of parent who will let a kid stick their hand in the socket if they still want to after I've told them not to do it a few times. If one of them comes in crying to me after touching a hot stove, after I've already told them not to do it, I will look at him closely and say, "I told you so," while getting some ice and a bandage for him. Sometimes kids need to experience the things we've already told them not to do just to fully realize the point.

If Boris is acting out, I'll raise my voice the first time and speak with a smile. If he pushes it again, he gets a warning that I seriously mean it. That usually does the trick. If he tries to get physical with me, as many young kids often do, I'll hold on to him until his urge passes. I'll tell him Big J. doesn't do time-outs, Big J. does knockouts. Hmm, maybe there's more of my mother in me than I thought.

Arthur's parents, Marie and Olivier, keep a swear jar in their home. I think this is a good idea for any house-

*birthday celebration
with dr. alex.*

hold. There are always better ways to express yourself than cussing. (Maybe I should suggest a swear jar to Tyra for the girls' house on *ANTM*.) Every time someone says a swear word they have to put one euro in there. There's a list on the side of the glass that has all the words that aren't allowed—*piss, shit, f**k, ass,* the usual. One morning we woke up and noticed that the word *Arthur* had been added to it. When we confronted him about it, he said, "I'm tired of people always saying, 'Arthur, do this,' and 'Put that down, Arthur,' and '*No,* Arthur.'"

171

Smart kid, that one. They both are. They're so well-behaved when we take them out places, especially when we all go shopping together. Speaking of shopping (sorry, dear readers, I know that segue was about as smooth as a crocodile clutch), this book wouldn't be complete if I didn't throw in a few words of wisdom about the topic. While I still create as many of my own clothes as possible, just because I enjoy it, I've spent more than enough time in stores during my life to pick up some tips to share.

There are a few classics and basics that should always remain in your closet, even if you're doing a major overhaul and getting rid of as much as you can. Every woman should have a simple sheath dress in navy, gray, or black. You can always throw a cardigan over it for work and then take it off for an evening cocktail. The two items it's always good to invest in are bathing suits and shoes. With bathing suits, it's probably the one time a woman is most critical about herself, so it's fine to splurge on one that makes you feel fantastic. With shoes, if you happen to find a pair of heels that are actually comfortable to walk in, then by all means spend what they're asking, because it's a rare find. Also, a gorgeous bag is worth spending a lot of money on because even if you don't have any cash left to put in it, you can rock a good bag with anything. It distracts the eye. Tyra tells girls to smile with their eyes; I like to smile with my handbag.

I love a girl who knows what kinds of outfits look great on her, but not everyone is born with that instinct. No problem. If you have a full bosom and some hips and a small waist, the fifties is a great era to get inspiration for clothes from, since this body type was then quite popular. A thin waist, like you find on pencil skirts, is quite sexy. If you have a short neck, you want to do a little lower neckline, so you don't lose it. A skinny waifish girl can go for a lot of looks, because she's basically a hanger. She can make anything look longer and thinner. *But* she needs a fit that isn't too tight, something that hugs at the hip and gives her a little bit of shape, so she doesn't look like one half of a set of parallel lines. A woman who is curvy wants a cut that lays on the hip and isn't too tight. The perfect outfit is a dress that's fitted in the shoulders and fits to the hip but is not too tight. Ask a tailor (if you have a good one) or the store to make alterations. And this goes for women of all shapes—if you find something that you love and feel really sexy and comfortable in, buy it in as many different colors as you can. I think that's very, very important. You can then change up the look with shoes, jackets, and accessories.

Be careful of a salesperson who thinks that everything you try on looks beautiful on you. That's when you know you're being bullshitted. Your friends will be the best judge. They'll tell you if what you are trying on looks terrible or is unflattering in the butt. And that should go both ways. If you can't tell a friend when something looks bad on *her*, then who will tell you when you're wearing something awful? As my friend Michael Stein once said to a friend, "If you don't want to know the truth, don't ask that evil black bitch, because he would tell you the truth and hurt your feelings. He's not going to sugarcoat it." But I'd *rather* tell you if something looks terrible on you. It's hard to say, "Oh my God, that looks amazing," when your friend looks like a potato sack in their new dress. I once told one model, a Dutch girl, that the dress she'd just bought didn't fit right. My exact words were, "I think it could look nicer; it's making your shoulders look strange."

"But do you like the dress?" she pressed.

"You bought a dress that you like, but it doesn't look good on you," I told her.

We can't wear everything. There are a lot of things I would love to wear, but my body doesn't have the right shape. There are outfits I've loved, but I knew I'd probably look like a piece of black asphalt laying in front of a driveway if I wore them. After the model left, her friend said to me, "I can't believe you said that to her. You could have just lied and told her she looked nice; now you made her feel self-conscious."

"No," I replied, "I made her feel conscious about when she goes shopping to try something on and making sure it's going to look good on her body before she buys it." It's about being honest. I didn't say it to be mean; the dress just didn't look right and it didn't give her the shape that she needed. The key to telling this sort of truth is all in the delivery. You have to make sure you don't sound condescending or cruel and make sure to tell your friend that you hope she would be just as honest with you. Sometimes the truth hurts. If you are really serious about your look and a die-hard fashion addict, then remember, the rule is style over comfort.

CHAPTER NINE

SPIRIT IN THE SKY

I used to think that you had to be inside of a church in order to pray, so later in life it was sort of a revelation for me to realize that you can pray sitting on a bus. As humans, we tend to go to God for every little thing under the sun. We're always begging, *Please, God, let me win the lottery, let me pass my English exam, let me get into college, make him fall in love with me,* and so on. I think that's ridiculous. I pray in order to still be a part of what the universe has to offer. Really though, spirituality is whatever *you* make it out to be. The great thing about spirituality is that it is yours and yours alone, and no one can take it away from you. As I got older, God, spiritual-

ot a tattoo? Make sure to cover it with sunblock so it doesn't fade or turn gray. Use a facial moisturizer with SPF if you don't want to smell like the beach (even though I love that smell sometimes).

ity, and a higher being all seemed to go hand in hand. It began to mean something very different to me than the typical Bible stories I learned while going to church with my grandmother. Basically, I believe that somewhere in the universe is a spirit that helps guide you when you're in touch with your soul. And sometimes even when you aren't.

I have a recurring dream where I'm back in our old apartment in the Castle Hill housing project, talking to my grandmother from another room. Her back is always to me and I very rarely see her face (I'm sure a dream analyst would have a field day with that one), but whenever I wake up I feel very clear and focused about my life. Sometimes I can smell a hint of lily of the valley when a soft breeze blows by, even if I'm in a place where there are no flowers to be found within a three-mile radius. Whenever that happens, I know it's my grandmother coming around to let me know that everything is going to be okay with whatever I'm going through or about to go up against. And there have been *a lot* of times in my life when I've needed that sense of warmth and security.

When I was a young man out discovering myself while partying in New York City's club scene, my friends and I started hearing whispers about some sort of strange gay cancer. The rumors that flew around back then were ludicrous. I kid you not—the first time I heard the word *AIDS* was when someone was telling me that only green monkeys and Africans could catch it. Maybe *green monkey* was some sort of racist terminology I wasn't aware of, but I took it literally. I figured since I wasn't African and I wasn't a green monkey I had nothing to worry about. When I heard that an acquaintance had died of pneumonia, I thought, *Damn fool boy went out in the cold barefoot,* because my mother had always said, "Put some damn shoes on before you catch your death of pneumonia." When I first heard the term *HIV-positive,* I thought it was a good thing, because the classification had the word *positive* in it. But the whisperings got louder, and sometimes someone would walk into a club looking particularly skinny. The rumors would race through the club—*she's got it.*

Once I figured out the real details, I made sure to keep myself safe and got tested regularly. But it made terror enter the bedroom. I'd be scared that a tiny bit of contagion had gotten in my eye, or maybe I had a paper cut I didn't know about.

One of the greatest loves of my life was a married man with a family. Let's call him Laurent. We were together for some time, on and off, in a relationship full of pointless drama. It started out as just a few random hookups, in between which we didn't see each other for long periods of time. But after a while we grew closer. I ended up meeting his children and his parents, and he even asked me to move in with him. I wasn't about to give up my own apartment, but I did move some things over to his house. As soon as this happened, all sorts of red flags started waving. Whenever I'd walk into a room and he was on his computer he would quickly close his screen, but not before I noticed that he was looking at websites that seemed to have a lot of rainbow flags and flesh tones on them. One time Laurent was leaving for a business trip and he wouldn't tell me where he was staying. While he was showering and getting ready to leave, I peeked inside his suitcase and found a bunch of condoms. I felt sick to my stomach but I didn't confront him about it. As soon as he was gone I looked through his apartment for any other signs that he was cheating on me, and I got way more than I bargained for. I discovered naked photos of him, letters from young men asking him for money, and worst of all, his little black book. It was actually just a bunch of papers, maybe twenty-five in all, listing names of guys, where he'd met them, whether he'd paid for sex, and the method of transportation used to get to the date. They were the metaphorical bedpost notches of an obsessive-compulsive Taurus, and my name appeared somewhere in the *middle* of the list. Be careful what you look for, you may not like it.

Memories suddenly flooded back to me about chastising him for openly ogling young guys on the sidewalk. It had always made me feel insecure, but I stayed with him because I was so in love.

On one of his trips out of town, he had a bad car accident. He invited me to his brother's house in Lille, where he was recuperating with a broken leg and some other injuries. I felt so terrible that he had been hurt, and we ended up sleeping together on his sickbed, with his cast on and everything. He came back to Paris about two weeks later and stayed at his ex-wife's apartment because she had a stall shower he could use to bathe in. He was eventually well enough to return to his own apartment, even though it took him forever to climb up five flights of stairs with his crutches. Ever since the accident we'd been closer than ever and I was excited to take care of him. I was hoping that maybe his injury had put the fear of death in him and that maybe he wanted to settle down for good with me.

I got him all comfortable on the sofa and helped him strip down to his underwear because it was so hot, and the cast just made it worse for him. Once he was settled, he looked at me and said, "I want to say something to you. Can you bring me a glass? I need to have a drink." He poured himself some scotch and looked at me. I thought he was going to tell me he had decided finally that I was the one for him.

"I'm positive," he said.

My heart soared for a moment. He was positive about us! I was the one! We were going to be together forever!

"I'm HIV-positive," he elaborated. My whole body froze, and then it began to crumble. "Please don't cry," he said. "I need you strong for me."

I was convinced that I already had HIV in that moment, but I stopped my panic long enough to tell him that I wasn't going anywhere and that I would take care of him. And a small part of me thought this might be the thing that would finally bring us together for good. I would get to be his caretaker.

Laurent had found out his status while he was in the hospital right after the car accident. I knew I needed to get tested. I was so incredibly scared. I pictured all of the skinny and sick people I remembered from the early days of the epidemic. I thought my career would be over, that I would turn into one of those walking skeletons I

WALK THIS WAY:

Sometimes You Need To Cry

*H*ave a lot of pent-up emotion? Need to get it all out with a good cry, but your body just won't cooperate? Watch a few episodes of *Extreme Makeover: Home Edition.* Guaranteed to turn even the hardest of hearts into a blubbering mess.

remembered from the past. After a four-month debate in my head, I got my blood tested. I had to wait one week for the results. During that week I imagined the worst. I mentally chose ten friends who I would tell. I couldn't sleep for days. In the middle of the night I'd stare up at the darkened ceiling.

The day I was to go and get my results back, it was dreary outside. *This is it,* I thought. *It's gray outside, a death sentence.* All the way to the clinic I thought of all the people in my life I'd known who AIDS had claimed. So many of my friends from the early days of going out were now gone. I listed their names one by one in my head and got up to sixteen people before my heart became so heavy that I could no longer take it. I made a right turn and went past the church St. Eustache. Right as I was walking by it, the clouds parted briefly and a rainbow appeared. A shiver went through me and I thought maybe it was a sign. By the time I got to the doctor, though, it was miserable and dark again. I sat in his office waiting for him to return with my results. I wanted nothing more than to see that rainbow again, so I stood up and looked out the window. There were the beautiful Palais Royal gardens below, and I said to myself, *If the sun comes out right now, everything is going to be all right.* And just like that, the garden was suddenly flooded with sunlight from the parting clouds. The colors around the garden went from gray to butter yellow to coral orange and I just *knew* everything was going to be okay. Just then the doctor entered with my file and told me that everything was fine. I was negative.

I thought of everything I'd done in bed for the past ten years. I always had good intentions but sometimes condoms break, sometimes someone has bloody gums they don't know about. Pay attention, because these aren't concerns that only gay men need to worry about.

Laurent and I stayed together but it was still never

considered "official," and after a while it seemed like he was starting to resent me and then just flat-out not like me at all. In the end, he just plain didn't want me. I hadn't even let on that I knew he was up to his old tricks, still sleeping around with lots of young guys. It made me furious because I didn't know if he was being safe. He certainly hadn't been safe with me after finding out that he was positive, that time at his sister's house. He finally broke it off for good with me after a terrible weekend out at a house in Normandy he owned. He had also invited three other couples there for a dinner party and spent the whole time ignoring me and making it obvious he wished I wasn't there. We had a massive blowout that even got physical, and in the end his exact words were, "I want to end this story." So he drove me to the train station, and the story ended—with my keys scratching grooves along the entire right side of his brand-new cobalt blue Mercedes. Bastard.

Despite attending so much church with my grandmother when I was young, it isn't something that I do on a regular basis now. When I remember, I do pray. I just say the basic stuff, thanking him for the things he's given me, acknowledging the things he has taken away and coming to terms with that. I thank him for everything he's given me, for guiding me, for keeping me here, and I

WALK THIS WAY:

Breaking Up Is Hard To Do

*t*he song says it all. I initially leaned on my friends for support and rehashed the story so many times that they finally had to tell me to snap out of it and move on with my life. It was the best advice they could have given me. I knew I needed to make a clean break, so I gave away every single thing that belonged to him and anything he had ever given me. And I mean *everything*—from an expensive watch to crappy old wooden pencils. I think it's better to get rid of it all because it makes it that much harder to move on if you don't. Say you find someone new and you're just starting to fall in love; maybe you're making out for the first time, and you come up for air and the first thing your eye lands on is that stupid Hallmark teddy bear your ex gave you, the one that says I WUV U on its belly. Perfect way to kill the mood.

bless others around me. When I'm acknowledging people who have died I try to go in chronological order. Sometimes that can take a while! I don't ever ask for things, and as I said before, I don't believe people should. It just seems terribly rude to ask God for material possessions. It's better to let those sorts of things come to you as a result of your own hard work, or sometimes even by chance, if you learn how to give up control. In a lot of cases I *had* to learn by force to give up control, to just let things go and let the universe take care of things.

For a long time I had been bouncing around from apartment to apartment in Paris, and I really just wanted to settle down and have a place to call home that I knew was mine, one where I didn't have to worry about suddenly being evicted because of a crazy roommate or a shady landlord. I had a photographer friend named Tierney Gearon who had an apartment in Paris that she told me she wanted to get rid of. When I went to see it, I recognized it. I had been to a dinner party there a few years earlier. It was where I first met Kate Moss. Tierney was moving to London and was looking for someone to take over her lease for a year and a half. I decided to sublet it and I paid my rent directly to Tierney.

The apartment building was classically French—meaning that it was old and lopsided and lacked most of the essentials that Americans take for granted, like a stove. When you entered you'd walk into a small foyer. The bathroom was to the immediate left and the kitchen was next to that. Straight ahead was a long hallway lined on both sides with all of my shoes, like a garden pathway framed with beautiful flowers. At the end of the hallway were two bedrooms and the living room.

I decorated it with a hodgepodge of items that friends had given me. There was a mix of mismatched used furniture, including a table with glass mirror tops on it that I covered in fabric so it didn't look like I was living in some sort of coke den. There was an oatmeal-colored three-cushion couch I had inherited from Sherry Gordon, another model. I had loads of plants because I have an excellent green thumb. When plants come into my life, they bloom and grow like crazy. I had stacks and stacks of magazines all over the chairs, mostly all of the international editions of *Vogue* and more-underground titles like *The Face* and *V.* The only lighting was one big halogen lamp. I made drapes for the windows out of burlap. The ones in the kitchen were blue, the pairs in the bedrooms were beige, and I used orange for the living room. In my room I had a futon mattress without the frame on the floor that I'd sleep on without unfolding it completely. If I had a guest for the evening I pulled it all the way out. Next to the bed was a window and a wall, where I attached a four-tier rack and put my clothes on it—stacked shirts, T-shirts, and sweaters. Another clothing rack held all my suits, pants, jackets, and coats.

I needed a roommate and found a photographer named Jonty Davies, who has since then gotten quite huge. He shot the Victoria's Secret campaigns for the last couple of years. He built a platform bed in his room, and he would let me store things underneath. In the kitchen I had a small broiler oven and a small two-burner stovetop that I had to go buy huge tanks of gas for when they ran out. I'd lug the big canisters back to the apartment by myself. I was always terrified that I was going to blow one up whenever I was attaching it to the burner. But then I realized, *If I get blown up, I get blown up. Stick the damn thing in and be done with it.* After that, I wasn't afraid anymore.

There were so many things I would have loved to have in that apartment. I was always falling in love with furniture and wallpaper prints that I saw in stores, but they were items that were impossibly out of my budget. I would go to visit my friends' homes and think, *This is a really nice place; I want everything in it for myself!* So, just like I had done with clothing when I was a teenager, I learned how to create the things I was coveting.

Take Pictures Of Other People's Spaces

*i*f you're staying at a fancy hotel or visiting a wealthy friend and you see furniture or a bedspread or curtains or anything else that you like, take a photo of it and start keeping an archive for inspiration. I always take pictures of hotel rooms I stay in now. You'd be surprised how easy it is to re-create things like headboards with some fabric, foam, a piece of wood, and a staple gun. If you're spatially challenged, you can use the pictures to help you get an idea of how to properly place furniture in rooms to maximize space and light. ◢

One day, after about six months of living in the apartment and working my butt off to make it a home that was truly my own, I was lying on the futon going through the mail and I opened an official-looking document written in French. This was before I had learned the language well and thus I couldn't understand what it said. So I took it to the accountant at Elite, who translated it for me. Basically, the building owner wanted me to prepare to receive prospective new residents, because the owner wanted to sell the apartment. I was angry and annoyed because she had told me I could have it for a year and a half, but more than anything I was sad and a little scared. I'd worked hard to turn that apartment into a really nice place. But she turned everything over to the real-estate office. I wrote a letter to the owner explaining the situation. She was surprisingly sympathetic, considering I was a subletter, but the only help she could offer was to say I could buy the place if I wanted it. But of course I couldn't afford to do that. It was such a far-flung idea that it had never even entered my mind. A mortgage was incomprehensible and I knew nothing about owning property. All I knew how to own was a runway. All I'd ever hoped for was an apartment with my name actually on the lease. But since I was a foreigner, that had always been impossible. Landlords didn't want to rent to me; they were afraid I would run out in the middle of the night or just not ever pay the rent.

I started to have anxiety attacks. I was always hyperventilating, I couldn't sleep, I couldn't focus. I started to hoard all of my money, not knowing where I was going

You Must Relax!

i would be nowhere in this world if I hadn't learned the extremely important value of using healthy self-esteem and generous doses of confidence to my advantage. You really do have to fake it to make it, and that requires holding your head high and walking forward like you mean it. But the stuff doesn't grow on trees. Confidence is greatly increased when you feel good about yourself! Here are five easy, inexpensive ways to treat yourself like a rock star in order to feel like one.

■ Eat healthfully. If it's true that you are what you eat, then you are doing yourself no favors by gorging on that McDonald's cheeseburger and fries. It's amazing how often people forget to eat simple fruits and vegetables on a daily basis.

■ Pamper yourself. Take a long warm bath with some relaxing essential oils (lavender has soothing properties) whenever you get a chance. Invest in an aromatherapy shower gel if you're seriously time crunched.

- Meditate. Whether you prefer to do this within the privacy of your own home or in a yoga studio alongside others, clear ten minutes to rebalance yourself each day.

- Avoid toxic people. I don't care if they're family or friends. If you surround yourself with negativity, it will creep into your psyche. Anger is contagious! Luckily, the opposite is true when you have access to loving, positive people.

- Read a book. Okay, clearly you're already all up on this. So keep in mind that reading is not only inspirational, it's a quiet, relaxing activity that gets you away from the chaos of everyday life!

to end up. I'd finally found somewhere to keep all of my things in one place and call my very own. I had my own set of keys and could come and go whenever I wanted to; I didn't have to worry about waking up someone I'd been staying with because they'd locked the door on me. I didn't have to worry about eating food in the fridge and wondering if it was mine. All of these things that I'd longed for had finally come true and now it was going to be taken away.

The anxiety eventually got to be way too much. So one night I lay down on my futon, and thought, *Why am I getting upset?* I stretched out in the dark, staring at the blackened ceiling. The only light I saw was a dim yellow streak coming in from the street. I started to talk to myself out loud.

I walked myself through each step. I was upset because I had finally found an apartment that I could call my own, and now I was being told that I had to move. I didn't ever want to have to move again; I'd been moving my entire life, bouncing from one place to another, sometimes even just staying on friends' sofas. So I asked myself *why* exactly was I so upset that I had to move again. I'd certainly done it enough times; it wasn't like I didn't know how to do it. Was it just because it was annoying to have to pack everything and move someplace else again? That was really the worst *physical* outcome. Deep inside I knew it was because I was tired and I just wanted my own place finally, an apartment I could be responsible for, a place that would be waiting for me when I returned home from traveling all over the world.

But it didn't look like this was going to be that place for me after all. So I said to myself, "Well, that's it. Let it go. If you're supposed to have it, you'll have it."

The next day a small note arrived, again written in French. I figured it was going to tell me the date I needed to be out by, so I got out my little French-to-English dictionary and translated it. It read: "The apartment is okay for you to rent, please come in to sign the papers." I thought I was misunderstanding it, that I must have translated it wrong and they were expecting me to come down and put a bid on owning the place. I took the note down to Elite again and the accountant told me, "No, J., it says you can stay in the apartment if you just sign a lease of your own."

I couldn't believe it. Right after I'd finally given up control and left the situation up to fate, fate did right by me. And I knew because this had happened that I was ready to take the responsibility.

I ended up staying in that apartment for seven years. After that period of time, the owner of the apartment

Sometimes You Just Gotta Leave It Up To Fate

*t*he interesting thing about prayer and the idea of fate is that it always seems to work best when you have a backup plan waiting in the wings in case things don't go your way. The idea that God helps those who help themselves really does work. The operative word there is *work.* You have to be willing to work hard, and if you do, other people aren't going to be the only ones who notice. The universe does, too. I don't know how to put it much plainer. It has always worked that way in my life and in my friends' lives as well. Complaining and bitching about your situation will get you nowhere in life. No one wants to hear it, least of all a higher power who has got more important things to do than listen to somebody whine without taking any action. ⚞

decided she wanted to sell for real this time. I was doing better financially but still wasn't in a position to buy property, despite her offering me right of first refusal. Once again, fate intervened.

During my seven years in the apartment, the one below me had a steady stream of tenants moving in and moving out. They'd come and go constantly, like sewer rats. There were always anywhere from four to six different people living down there.

There was another batch of tenants leaving around the same time that I found out I had to move, so I grabbed one and asked him what was up. He was moving back in with his parents in the south of France, and I asked him for the number of the owner of that apartment. So I called him up and explained my situation. He came by to check out my place and saw how neat and clean and in order it was, a far cry from the usual mess of his space below. He thought about it for a minute and agreed to let me move in on one condition. He'd give me a deal on the rent if I agreed to fix the place up. Basically, he wanted me to correct the damage that years of bad tenants had done to it. We came up with a sketchy agreement where I paid him half the rent in cash under the table and half by check. But I didn't care, because I still had my name on the lease, so I couldn't get tossed out.

It took me three days just to get the grease off of the walls of the kitchen so that a fresh coat of paint could stick to it. I was cleaning up the grime of at least fifty different people who had lived in that apartment. Most of them were students, which should give you some sort of idea what I was up against. I pulled up dirty carpets, redid the floors, and painted everything. I put in new cabinets and a brand-new countertop—my ex-boyfriend Alex sent his parents in Slovakia the measurements and they had a gorgeous marble countertop made for me for nothing. They drove twenty-one hours in their car to deliver it.

The landlord initially told me he would give me one year to fix the whole place, but I had the entire apartment done within three months and lived there for another seven years. All in all, I spent fourteen years in that same building, the longest I'd ever lived in one place for my entire life.

CHAPTER TEN

CHANGES

Madonna and Linda Evangelista aren't the only ones who get to be the queens of reinvention. It's easy for them—in pop culture and fashion you can always change yourself just by dying your hair or losing (or gaining) a few pounds. But for the rest of us it takes a bit more work. If things are going good in your life, then don't sweat it. I'm fond of saying "If it ain't broke, don't fix it." But sometimes a tune-up is necessary and change needs to be made. The best way to tell if that needs to happen is to gauge your mood. And you do that by asking yourself one simple question: Are you happy?

Sometimes you have to reinvent yourself just to keep

Four Ways To Get Off Your Butt Now!

*L*ook, everyone gets in a rut now and then, be it wearing the same jeans five days in a row because they're the only ones that fit right or making a habit out of coming home from work and watching TV for three hours straight. The fact is, it's really hard to make even small changes in your routine. Here are five ways to get moving in a new direction and make monotony so last year.

- Make a list. What are you passionate about? You know those lists of interests people fill out on online profiles (origami, yoga, horseback riding, stuff like that)? Half the time, they aren't actively involved in any of them on a regular basis. If this sounds familiar to you—and you *know* it does—reevaluate what's important to you in order to identify any personal loves you've been missing out on.

- Take up a cause. If you're concerned about homeless animals, why not start volunteering to play with cute dogs on the weekend? (See, that doesn't sound so bad, does it?) You may even end up with a new best friend.

- Get a hobby. If the wool you bought two years ago because you thought you'd take up knitting is still sitting in your junk drawer, take it out and get moving on it already. Even better, join a group of like-minded individuals so you can not only meet people but also have the added bonus of extra motivation.

- Start exercising. Speaking of getting motivated, I know this one can be hard, it really can, but here's my suggestion: Bust out your "skinny pants." Immediately. Do they fit? Nah, didn't think so. The cool thing about working out on a regular basis (besides fitting into those fabulous trousers) is that you'll get such an amazing energy boost that trying new things will start to come naturally. ◢

up with the world around you. Take technology, for example. I resisted getting a laptop or a cell phone for years. I didn't want the extra weight of carrying around a computer in my bag and I thought cell phones would give me face cancer. Combined, I figured I'd end up glowing in the dark. Now it's ten years later and I have a panic attack if I'm staying in a hotel room that doesn't have a wireless Internet connection or if I wander into a dead zone. I need to check out the latest photos from the Milan shows! I need to make sure my name is on the list!

Fashion itself embodies the very idea of reinvention. There are very few new ideas left in fashion. All of it is borrowed from other people's shapes, fabrics, and trimmings from years past. Since I could never afford new clothes when I was younger, I was constantly learning new tricks on my sewing machine in order to keep current.

On *America's Next Top Model* we are constantly reinventing the contestants, most obviously and noticeably on the infamous makeover episodes. I'll be the first to admit that sometimes what we choose isn't the best look for the girl. One reinvention that does always work is when a girl who has spent her whole life hiding her face behind her long hair gets all of her hair cut completely off. We're forcing her to confront the world, to reinvent herself into someone who can stare the world in the eyes and feel comfortable letting the world stare back. The ones who are able to handle it always go far. The physical reinvention begets the mental one.

I'm always really excited when I run into an *ANTM* girl a year after I've last seen her and she has managed to reinvent herself yet again. I love it when I don't even recognize her. That's when I feel like we're really accomplishing something with the show. We've given her the tools and the confidence to try new things.

My confidence stems from the fact that as soon as I realized it was possible, I started living my life the way I wanted to. I didn't give one shake of an arm full of Cartier bracelets what people thought of me. From age twelve on I had no interest in following the crowd. Despite working at Payroll Procedures, I knew I didn't want to work a normal nine-to-five job. I got my wish, times ten. Sometimes I end up working from nine AM to five in the morning.

I knew in my own eyes (and was told by many others) that I did not fit the ideal of what a young black man should look like—certainly not what a young black male *model* should look like. The accepted idea of beauty for black models when I was growing up was someone with light skin, wavy hair, not-so-full lips. I had none of those. Everyone says beauty is in the eye of the beholder and

Get A Nose Job If You Really Want It

*a*t this point in history everyone knows that fashion is all smoke and mirrors. We're selling fantasy and dreams. Unfortunately there are still people who see fashion images as an ideal to aspire to. I've watched women walk into Barney's with a photo of Naomi Campbell and tell the staff, "I want to look like this." They want the exact same hair, smile, earrings, dress, and shoes. Usually they end up looking like clowns. But nowadays, if a woman decides she wants the same smile, ass, and breasts as Naomi Campbell, she can buy that, too. I say if it makes you feel better about yourself, go for it. But if I had gotten my wish about wanting to be white when I was a kid, I don't think there's any chance I'd be where I am today. Chew on that for a bit before you book a consultation.

that beauty is only skin deep. I knew all that and was lucky enough to have the self-confidence to pursue modeling anyway, but let's face it, we live in a world where people are mostly judged by their outward appearance. With the exception of writers, radio announcers, and phone sex operators, people's idea of you is formed based on a visual before anyone takes the time to talk to you and get to know you on the inside. But I knew that I had a gift inside that was much more perfect and beautiful than physical beauty, and it's called talent. Being aware of that made me able to go with the flow and take on pretty much anything that was handed to me. I can take a woman, no matter how tall, short, fat, or thin, and make her move with personality and confidence. Going back to the lesson I learned at Bergdorf, always feeling secure about asking questions made me feel smarter and more confident, too. I never felt like I had to hide anything and it makes me able to understand each individual client and their needs. If you doubt yourself because of how you think you look physically, the best way to build up confidence is to recognize your talents and look for a way to make a living off of them, because being happy with your career will make you believe in yourself, and the more you believe in yourself, the more beautiful you become.

I know most modeling agencies will tell you otherwise, but I firmly believe that size doesn't matter when
it comes to being a model. If you're short, you may not
be able to do runway, but you can always do beauty and
editorial. When I was modeling for thirty minutes, I
certainly didn't have the kind of body you'd normally as-
sociate with someone who does runway. Or at least a

Setting Goals

i'm an Aries, so I like to plan things in advance. And while it's important to set goals for yourself, you have to make sure your goals don't become your entire identity. When I was a kid I never thought I'd be living the life I do now. I was lucky enough to have things keep coming my way that I wanted to do because I stayed in the field that I love. And once I was in it, I said yes to anything that came my way that seemed interesting and new. If you think you're off track in life, set small goals to keep yourself moving forward but watch that you don't lose yourself in your drive or ambition. I think that what tends to happen a lot is a person will become so wrapped up in their goals that they will become hardened and not very nice because of their desperation to climb to the top. Make sure that you leave time for friends and family and love while you pursue your dreams, because if you don't, once you've achieved what you wanted, it will be a hollow victory. You'll have no one to share it with. ⌐

male model. I was a size zero minus 3.25 grams. I could wear a sample size of any dress, but I also wanted to have muscles. But muscles don't look good in a dress. I would always wear sweaters that covered my ass, because I thought I didn't have a butt. I would stretch my shirts and pull them down over my knees to hide the fact that I thought I had a nonexistent rear end. The point is everyone has body issues, even models. Especially tall black men who want big muscles but model dresses.

There is one little girl in my life, the daughter of a close friend, named Blanche. Blanche is eight years old and a bit heavy. This may be the norm in America, but in France, she attends school with a classroom full of lithe and petite little French girls. Blanche knows that she has inherited her father's genes. He's a bit short and stocky himself. Not unhealthy or overweight, mind you, it's just the way he is built. For an eight-year-old though, Blanche has a pretty mature understanding about her body weight and what is healthy and what is not. What I like to do is cook for her and her family as often as possible (I'm actually a great chef; bet you didn't know that!) and make healthy options for her to eat. I don't want her to feel bad for asking for seconds when she sees her siblings doing the same thing, so what I and her mother do is give her a first helping that is only half of what everyone else is getting but arranged in such a way that no one can tell. Then when she asks for a second helping, we give her the other half, so in effect what she is getting is one full healthy portion. You can try any diet in the world, but the best way to go about losing weight is healthy eating, portion control, and exercise. When you feel good about yourself inside you will attract great people and energy around you. It's really that simple.

If you want to be in the fashion industry but really don't believe that you have the particular physical look that the modeling industry wants, don't let that stop you. There are so many different aspects of the fashion industry that you could go into that you might feel more comfortable in while still pursuing your passion—stylist, photographer, makeup artist, producer, PR director, designer, event planner, location scout, booking agent, magazine editor, fashion writer . . . the list goes on. Play on your strengths and interests. You're in charge of your own dreams—you have to be proactive.

If you're still in high school, don't worry about becoming popular, a cheerleader, or a homecoming queen. The truth is that practically everyone who makes it in the fashion industry was the school geek or weirdo. Lord knows I wore some crazy things at my school. In fact, if you're considered strange in your high school, your chances of surviving in the real world are much better than those of the "pretty" girl who is campaigning for head of the prom committee.

CHAPTER ELEVEN

THE END (FOR NOW)

I've talked a lot about models in this book—the fashion, the hard work, the walks, the history, the parties . . . frankly, I could go on forever about the subject. There is one particular kind of model that I hold in the highest regard though. This model is miles above the rest and leaves everyone in the dust. I'm talking about role models. (Bet you saw that one coming, didn't you?) Every fashion model worth her salt tries to align herself with a charitable cause, and that's great, but the true models in this world are the ones you won't see in a magazine or on the runway. They are the people who have stayed true to their beliefs, the ones who have over-

For extra-thick lashes, dip your finger in loose powder and gently rub it into your lashes (be careful to avoid getting any in your eye). Apply mascara as usual.

come great adversity, the neighbors who go out of their way to welcome the new family to the block. Even the smallest act of kindness resonates deeper within the universe than the shine from the brightest klieg light.

It's so easy to wrap yourself around the fantasy of the fashion world, but you have to remember that's all it is—a fantasy. If certain aspects of fashion make you feel good about yourself, then live it up. But a lot of people don't care about fashion at all, and that's just fine, too. I think it's horrific when someone I'm working with sneers at someone on the street whom they consider poorly dressed. For all they know, that person is a nurse who just got off a fourteen-hour shift of saving lives, and is just happy to be wearing a pair of comfortable shoes while she heads to the grocery store for her family.

The flip side of that scenario is a story nearly two hundred years old—that of the ugly duckling. Most people have probably been able to relate to that story at some point in their lives. (Anyone who says they haven't felt less beautiful than those around them at least once is probably lying to cover up a pretty big inferiority issue.) Sometimes I wish that that little duckling hadn't grown up to be the beautiful swan, and instead had learned how to value other aspects of himself first like intelligence, humor, and empathy in order to finally feel fulfilled. Sure, he suffered a lot of verbal and physical abuse and was finally able to come into his own physical beauty, and because of everything he suffered he knew he would never be mean to anyone, but wouldn't the lesson have been more powerful if the animals who had been mean to him eventually grew to love him just because he was a good-hearted creature?

I'm not sure we've evolved much since that story was written. In fact, we seem to be traveling backward. What's really sad and disgusting about our current culture is that for our entertainment, instead of investing in a movie or television show about something that is going to make us feel good, most people like to watch someone who is gorgeous on the outside and a horrible person with a mean streak on the inside. Just look at the success of shows like *The Bad Girls Club, Rock of Love, Flavor of Love, I Love Money,* etc. (Why do those shows insist on bastardizing the word *love*? They are about as far away from the concept of love as Arizona Jeans are from Helmut Lang.) It's sad that there are so many bad role models out there for young women. So many people on this planet feel entitled to everything without earning anything. They feel like if they have to do any small thing at all that they had better get something back in return. It's an awful way to think. You should never expect a favor back from someone if you do one first. But I've found that it *will* usually come back to you in some form or another.

One summer when I was a teenager I tried to get a job as a camp counselor. (Such a white-kid thing to do!) I didn't get the job, and a friend of mine told me later that she had heard the guy who ran the camp tell someone else it was because I was gay. My first thought was, *How did he know?* Looking back it was most likely the fact that at the interview I wore a T-shirt with a men's necktie tied around my waist, paired with tiny jean cutoffs with frayed edges and a peace sign cut into them. And sandals. But I didn't let that deter me. I believed in my clothing and outfits, and in the end, they were what helped open so many doors for me. If you really believe strongly enough in something and aren't willing to compromise, then don't. It might take you a little longer to get to where you want to go in life, but it will be worth it when you do. In a way, life is like one big go-see. Sometimes you get the job, the girl, the boy, the car, the house . . . and sometimes you don't. A model doesn't give up on her career after getting rejected at a go-see, and no one else in the world should quit their dreams because of a round of rejections either. Rejection is something that everyone faces, usually many, many times during their life. I stood on a mountain of nos in order to get one yes.

Just like no model should have the exact same walk as another model, you should never aspire to have the same walk through life as another person. It's okay to want to be a doctor like your mother, but don't feel like you have to go about it in the exact same way she did. If you want to take a year off from college and travel, then go for it. Celebrate your interests and your quirks. It is your differences that make you special, that make people want to stand up and take notice of you.

If I had to verbally tell a model how to walk down a runway, say, over the telephone, I'd tell her that the act is much less physical than it is mental. You need to have confidence in yourself and believe that you can do it, because what you are thinking on the inside is usually *so* apparent on the outside. I'd tell her that she needs to keep her shoulders back, her head held high, to always look forward, to take strong and steady steps toward her destination. It's almost exactly the same advice I would give to a high school student who wanted to know how to get ahead in a field she was interested in pursuing. Your very existence is one big journey toward the unknown, and everyone should feel beautiful and proud while they are making that walk.

On that one day, so many years ago, when I wasn't allowed into the store on Madison Avenue, I could have easily let that moment get me down so low that I never walked with my head held high again. Perhaps I have my genes to thank that I didn't let it affect me. Maybe it's because of the way that I was raised. Maybe it's because I just had a particularly strong will or because the universe was giving me internal strength. In all likelihood it is probably a combination of all four. The best part is that all of those things are qualities that *everyone* has. Even if you were raised in the most abusive household and have deep issues because of it or your family's genes left you with something that is extremely difficult to live with, like a disease, you can still make that choice inside your head to have a strong will. If you don't feel it, *tell* it to yourself. *Make* your brain believe it.

Statistically, I had everything going against me during my development. I'm black, I'm gay, my family didn't have much money. I was a flamboyant exhibitionist in a pretty dangerous section of New York City. But look where I am today. I'm still walking down Madison Avenue, window-shopping, dressed in my finest, not caring what anyone else thinks of me. And there isn't a single store that won't let me inside. (Well, at least for now there isn't.) You can't ever let adversity keep you from believing in yourself. I don't think it's any surprise that often the brightest, most intelligent and caring people in this world are physically challenged, or came from a background that was steeped in poverty, or are living with a debilitating disease, or are caring for children who were born sick. A person who has seen and dealt with the darkest parts of life is sometimes the one who is the most capable of seeing the light as well. It's also no surprise that there are many people in the fashion industry who are extremely unsatisfied with their own lives. It's so much easier to hide behind the glamour than to face reality.

We all know that life is hard, that each of our own individual runways sometimes feels like someone poured engine oil all over it and we're all just scrambling to get back up on our feet, let alone make it another few steps. But all you have to do is what any strong model would do. You stand back up, put your game face on, and keep on walking.

ACKNOWLEDGMENTS

Thanks to all who played a part of this journey. It's a long list, but necessary.

To André Leon Talley: For getting me into my first Yves Saint Laurent couture fashion show at the Intercontinental Hotel in Paris July 1986 and for the friendship and endless fashion lessons that have continued since.

To Robert Duffy: For thirty-one years of friendship and who still calls me "Alex" for all the gifts.

To Marc Jacobs: For all the visual gifts past and present from your "coloring book" collection—Perry Ellis, Marc Jacobs, and Louis Vuitton.

To Alexander McQueen: For believing I was worth the talent to send a drawing of the dress and a pair of heels to teach the Swedish model how to walk for Givenchy that year, and a train ticket from Paris to London to coach another model two years later.

To Mesh Chhibber: For bringing me to the John Galliano kingdom to coach a few beauties just before showtime.

To John Galliano: For keeping fashion and theater alive and allowing me to sit through hours of hair and makeup creative to help inspire the new girls walking for your show.

To Odile Gilbert: For allowing me to sit in the Atelier in Paris and watch for hours and hours as you researched, prepared, and created magic coiffures.

To Marcelino Gonzalez: For thirty years of loyal friendship, a few good hairdos, and sharing the right side of your bed on 15th and 16th Street.

To Orlando Pita: For years of friendship and years of creative fashionable visual hair madness and the gifts of leftover hair and accessories to help me create my own madness.

To Donald Scott: The first white boy to introduce me to my first hair relaxer and blow dry at the Donald Scott Salon. Ouch! That burned but the results were silky fabulous.

To Carlos de Souza from Valentino: For believing in my backstage walking lessons and tips to recommend the marriage between designer, agent, model, and me.

To Lars Nilsson: For constant lessons on talent, discretion, and loyal friendship.

To Monique Pillard: For introducing me to Hitomi.

To Oscar Reyes, Elite Model Management, NY: For allowing me to play "Millie the Model" at their offices and Christmas parties.

To Maurice Graham: For those fierce home cooked meals up on the Grand Concourse in the Bronx.

To John Casablancas: For giving me my first Elite Model Look competition in Seoul, Korea.

To Gerald Marie: For saying I should get paid for the talent and advice I gave so freely, and giving me my first runway lesson paycheck at Elite Paris.

To Gilles Murat: For allowing me to rent your wonderful daylight studio and home in Paris for years to teach, coach, and see many new models tear, fear, stumble, and tumble and become top runway divas. What would I have done without you?

To the agents past and present—Caroline Pedrix (Paris), Alex Schwab (Paris), Hitomi Shigeta (Japan), Laila Snellman (Finland): For believing in this freak of nature when others looked and said, "What the f&#k?!"

To Katerina Jebb: For being my survival partner in the small studio apartment in Paris in the 3rd arrondissement and later in the larger apartment in the 17th arrondissement. We did that together and we survived.

To Brad Harryman: For giving me your studio apartment in Paris rent-free for one year. RIP.

To Patricia Hartmann (Constantino): For loaning me one year's rent deposit for my first apartment in Paris.

To Sherry Gordon: For giving me all of her old furniture, which I still have and recovered three times to furnish my three different apartments in Paris.

To Maggie Albertini: For opening my eyes to the French.

To Director Bunny Godillot: For my first small part in her French film, *Riches, belles, etc.*

To Christian Lacroix: For loaning me the lavender couture gown and opera coat for my final scene in *Riches, belles, etc.* at Place Vendome.

To director Fabienne Berthaud: For my second small part in her French film, *Frankie*, opposite Diane Kruger.

To Kathyll Carnegie: For suggesting at Giorgio Armani on Madison Avenue that I go see Jean Paul Gaultier at the casting in New York's Bergdorf Goodman that spring of 1986. Where are you?

To Khaled: For the gifts of the Versace wardrobe that I could not afford then and mostly still have—though they're now called vintage.

To Glenda Goss: For a year and a half on your couch that was always too short and painful for me to stretch my legs. But girl, a fabulous address: East 59th between 1st and Sutton.

To Carmina Marcial: For your black sofa bed with that metal bar and thin mattress that killed my back. But I was never cold or wet during the Christmas stays at London Terrace.

To Bob Puddicombe: For the cot in the kitchen on that one late Saturday night on West 24th Street . . . I forgive you. Lol.

To Gary Steinkohl: For the sofa on East 9th Street and the lesson that you never give up. Life's not that short. You have survived.

To Bert and Camille: For years of sharing the house on the Sporenstraat in Maastricht, Holland.

To Steven Minichiello: For keeping living in a fantasy world alive.

To Carlos Taylor: For being a friend through thick and thin and never stopping the vision years later.

To Dolly K. Morton: For supplying me with countless *Vogue* magazines so that I left the Castle Hill Avenue projects in *Vogue* drag fashion as you watched through the peephole in the door.

To Kimora Lee Simmons: For letting the world know it's OK to be loud, fabulous, and over the top with diamonds, furs, and luxury. But most of all for being a mom, kind, generous, and giving to those in need.

To Tyra Banks and *America's Next Top Model*: For making me bankable.

To Jay Manuel: For "the 3 W's": Where? What? Why?

To Russell Simmons: For supporting me and showing through your books and words how to watch my back from the boardroom to the streets.

To Yusef Williams: For keeping the hair and kitchen snatched to undetectable perfection.

To Leola Westbrook: For always giving a clear honest answer when needed.

To Anthony Dominici: I like you better now that we don't work together.

To David Raff: For a million gazillion rides all over Los Angeles from "Toast-Lax."

To Lee Gonzalez / Robb Dickehut: For always keeping me in the right direction and on the right track in Hollywood through words, laughter, and actions. God knows a girl can get lost.

To William Clark: For keeping "C.P." time not a myth but a reality. Lol.

To Anne Marie Horsford: For the Hollywood wisdom to introduce me to her—and now my—accountant.

To Karl Large: The accountant who straightened my black ass out!

To Aaron Kanter, aka "Aark": For being the manager and keeping it all in order.

To Malcolm Harris: For your endless friendship and our inspirational hours of walks and talks throughout Manhattan known as J and Malcolm's "walkersations."

To Nancy Giallombardo: For making fabulous high heels for my big ass size 13 hoofs to strut in!

To Big Chris Daniels: For showing me the difference between ducks and seagulls twenty-six years ago.

To Alfredo Rovira: For being the best salesman at Brooks Brothers and seeing the beginning of all of this in the Bergdorf Goodman employee cafeteria.

To Gil Belleran: For being "White Eckly" for twenty years.

To Rich, Joann, and Max Sullivan: For the years of basement storage between two houses and the introduction to Louis Icart.

To Joey Curcio: For all the free meals when dollars and coins where sparingly low while visiting New

York . . . but our spirits were always high with realness and laughter.

To Carol Lewis / Jennifer Brown: For the sewing lessons back in the day that created future drag draaaaaaaaaaama!

To Sandra Brown: For my very, very first introduction to a fashion show production, the Sandra Brown Fashion Experience, in the Bronx.

To Jaron Eames: For singing your heart out and letting me know that in 1978 it was OK for a man to wear a full length mink coat and jewels at 10 a.m. on a Tuesday morning to go buy milk at the corner store.

To Debbie Matenopoulos: For sticking up for me 1000% every single time. It's not a typo. I do mean 1000%.

To Hannu Kallio / Mika Salonen: Kitos! Kitos two weeks maximum.

To Nancy Josephson: For suggesting this book.

To Suzy Unger: For making it happen.

To Joshua Lyon: Without you my hours of talking would have been just that, undocumented talk.

To Gene Marcial: For putting me in front of your camera lens and making me your top model guinea pig all of these years. RIP.

To North "James" Rebis: Your were right, I should

have listened to you over the kitchen sink that day. White boys can do black hair too.

To Marcia Lewin: For that unforgettable life lesson with such few words.

And to all the people who have said horrible things and have not been nice to me in the past, present, and I'm sure future, thank you! People like you still exist in the world to make me feel more special than I already am.

To anyone that I may have forgotten, I'll get you in the next book!

And to my damn self . . . for putting up with myself . . . all these years.

J. Alexander

PHOTO CREDITS

ABOUT THE AUTHOR

J. Alexander has traveled around the world casting and coaching models for countless top designers. Now he is a television personality well known for his work as a runway coach and judge on *America's Next Top Model.*